21ST-CENTURY SMALLHOLDER

From window boxes to allotments:
how to go back to the land
without leaving home

Paul Waddington

Paul Waddington is the author of *Seasonal Food: a guide to what's in season when and why* as well as a newspaper columnist and professional writer. He takes a deep interest in food and environmental issues and grows vegetables, keeps bees and tries very hard to live sustainably in south London with his wife and two children.

TRANSWORLD PUBLISHERS
61–63 Uxbridge Road, London W5 5SA
a division of The Random House Group Ltd

RANDOM HOUSE AUSTRALIA (PTY) LTD
20 Alfred Street, Milsons Point, Sydney,
New South Wales 2061, Australia

RANDOM HOUSE NEW ZEALAND LTD
18 Poland Road, Glenfield, Auckland 10, New Zealand

RANDOM HOUSE SOUTH AFRICA (PTY) LTD
Isle of Houghton, Corner of Boundary Road and Carse O'Gowrie, Houghton 2198, South Africa

Published 2006 by Eden Project Books
a division of Transworld Publishers

A catalogue record for this book is available from the British Library.
ISBN 190391969X / 9781903919699

Art direction & design by Fiona Andreanelli (www.andreanelli.com)
Design assistance by Vanessa Bowerman (www.foliotypo.co.uk)
Illustrations by Gillian Blease (www.gillianblease.co.uk)
Garden designs pp. 32, 37, 41 by Simon Saggers
Table on p. 207 courtesy of Simon Fairlie
Printed in Great Britain by Mackays of Chatham plc, Chatham, Kent

1 3 5 7 9 10 8 6 4 2

Papers used by Eden Project Books are made from wood grown in sustainable forests. The
manufacturing processes conform to the environmental regulations of the country of origin.

21ST-CENTURY SMALLHOLDER

Paul Waddington

Acknowledgements

I would like to thank Susanna Wadeson, who decided that this book's time had come, and the rest of the team at Transworld and Eden who also made it happen: Sarah Emsley, Mike Petty, Fiona Andreanelli, Gavin Morris and Brenda Updegraff. Thank you too to Gillian Blease for the beautiful illustrations. Being a complete novice in so many of the subjects covered by the book I have many experts to thank: Simon Saggers, whose beautiful smallholding is an inspiration and whose garden designs in this book will hopefully inspire others; Simon Fairlie for his expert advice on smallholding; Michael and Julia Guerra, who show how to create abundance from small spaces; John Chapple, a bee guru; Tony York for his pig expertise and Caroline Muir for letting me get to know her urban chickens. Adrian Evans and Helen Stuffins were inspirational and instrumental in shaping my views on sustainability. Peter Harper from the Centre for Alternative Technology provided a pragmatic corrective to the less practical extremes of 'green' thinking. Biologist David Perkins showed how beautiful biodiversity can be created in the most urban of spaces; Penney Poyzer and Gil Schalom demonstrated how a Victorian house can become an eco-home and Will Anderson shared his experience of creating an eco-friendly house from scratch. Thanks are due as always to my agent Sappho Clissitt; and to my wife and sons Fiona, Finn and Fergus who were a source of joy and support throughout.

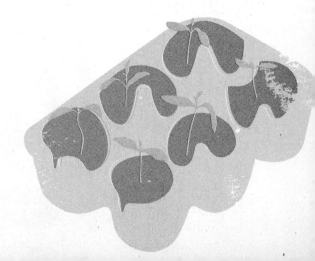

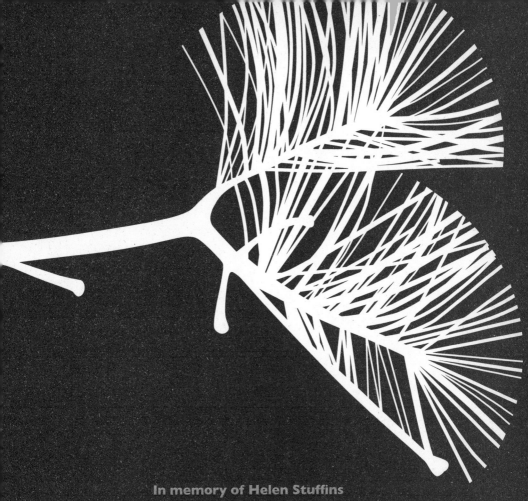

In memory of Helen Stuffins
a great inspiration and a great friend

CONTENTS

INTRO

Who wants to be a 21st-Century Smallholder?

Many of us dream of 'four acres and freedom' – the idyllic, self-sufficient life in which we flee the city to live in harmony with the land, dependent on no-one. For all but a fortunate few, this is now an impossible dream. Absurd property prices have put four acres and a farmhouse out of reach of anyone lacking a six-figure sum of capital. Today, only the rich can afford to be peasants.

But a way of life that reduces our impact on the planet whilst also improving our quality of life has never been more sorely needed. Look at any aspect of modern living and there's a very good reason for doing things differently.

The food we eat now comes from a handful of gigantic retailers. Their demand for an uninterrupted, year-round supply of cosmetically perfect produce is turning our countryside into an agribusiness factory. Our food chain is now entirely dependent on fossil fuels: first, to manufacture the pesticides and artificial fertilizers without which industrial agriculture fails; and second, to power agricultural machinery and the enormous, road-based transport infrastructure that delivers food from farmer to warehouse to supermarket. As Felicity Lawrence points out in the food industry exposé *Not on the Label*, just a few days without fuel would bring this country's food supply to a standstill.

So the modern food chain is insecure. It's also killing us: polluting the environment with runoff and residues, decimating biodiversity and – as we are now beginning to learn – giving us produce that is depleted in the minerals and micronutrients that make it worth eating in the first place. Is a lettuce that is grown with artificial fertilizer, slathered with pesticides, then chilled and trucked around the place for a few days before spending a week in the fridge going to be as good as the one just picked from your garden? The evidence suggests not; and intuition screams it. Growing your own is more than just a nice idea.

Then there's the way we use energy and resources. Our homes are responsible for a third of Britain's CO_2 emissions. Almost all are highly dependent on energy sources that are not only insecure and non-renewable but whose use is also – the evidence is now overwhelming – transforming our climate into something that could even become hostile to much of humanity in our lifetimes. It would take three planet Earths to support the entire world's population living as the British do. Thinking about reducing energy and resource dependence is no longer the preserve of the thrifty smallholder; it's something we could all benefit from, now and in the future.

Many of us dream of living differently because we can see what our Western lifestyles are doing to the environment. But I think we also aspire to peasantry because we instinctively feel that there is deep satisfaction to be gained from tasks that the consumer society would file under 'drudgery': growing and preserving food, animal husbandry, or managing your own water and energy resources. Our national fondness for gardening and pet ownership – scorned by nations that are closer to their pre-industrial pasts – surely points to a longing to be closer to nature. We have become 'de-skilled' since we industrialized, losing our ability to live off the land. Today, that de-skilling has accelerated as our needs have become provided

for by corporations. Even being a parent can be outsourced. In a generation, we've forgotten how to grow things, fix things, even cook from scratch. And we are all having to relearn about what food is in season when. If society collapsed tomorrow, only Ray Mears would survive. Skills that were once effortlessly handed down from generation to generation now have to be learnt through piles of books, lengthy courses or painful trial and error. But – as I have learnt – it's worth it. Few things beat the satisfaction of picking your own produce or knocking together your first beehive.

So perhaps we should all attempt to be self-sufficient at home in order to be healthy and happy and save the planet? I don't think so. Genuine self-sufficiency, in which you provide all your own material needs, is very, very tough. As the two case studies at the end of this book show, it requires a vast amount of learning, planning, investment and time, as well as a good-sized plot of land. If you had an immense garden, an iron will, accommodating neighbours and a complicit family, it might just be possible to emulate Tom and Barbara Good. Most of us aren't like this, though. And even if it were practical, I doubt whether widespread self-sufficiency is really desirable. For a start, it would put out of business the small-scale farmers who are finding new outlets for seasonal, local and often organic produce through farmers' markets and box schemes.

In between the Goods and the people who rampage from shopping mall to ready meal in a monster 4x4 is the 21st-Century Smallholder. You don't need four acres to be one; nor do you need vast amounts of capital and time. You won't be self-sufficient; but you'll grow and do the things that suit your home and your life. If you have a small flat, then maybe your window boxes could keep you in salads and herbs. If you have a small garden, perhaps you'll use part of it to grow gourmet fruit and veg that are best when just picked, and maybe have some chickens scratching around the place. And if you're fortunate enough to have a lot of outside space, then you may well be eating your own produce for much of the growing season; there might be bees . . . or even pigs. And wherever you live, you could be harvesting rainwater, making your own compost, saving – even generating – energy and turning your home into a wildlife haven.

Why be a 21st-Century Smallholder? There's a long list of good reasons: here are just a few. It's deeply satisfying. Whether it's your first home-grown salad, home-laid egg or solar-heated shower, there's a great sense of achievement to be had. Being a 21st-Century Smallholder also makes your house and garden look beautiful and attract wildlife. A productive fruit and veg garden is a nicer place to be than a desert of decking, both for you and for the countless bugs and creatures that run our ecosystem. If you grow and raise some of your own food and manage some of your own resources (like water and energy), it reduces your dependence on our damaging consumer culture. It may only be a token reduction – cutting yourself off from the mains, for example, is not something to be undertaken lightly – but it feels good; it feels like taking control in a world where the power to run one's day-to-day life is being reduced to nothing more than consumer choice. Finally, it's good to feel like part of the solution. Your water butt may not solve the world's freshwater crisis; your home-made compost may not save the peat bogs; and your solar panels might not stop the glaciers melting; but big changes start with lots of grassroots actions.

It doesn't have to take much time, or cost much money, to be a 21st-Century Smallholder. You can start growing fruit and veg on a shoestring budget; and many of the actions that most reduce your environmental 'footprint' are free and will save money. Solar electricity, big food-growing operations, 'eco-retrofitting' your house: these things do cost money. But there's something for everyone in the 21st-Century Smallholder's lifestyle. However far you want to go, this book is designed to help you along the way.

So how much of a 21st-Century Smallholder is the author? I'm getting there. I'm fortunate enough to have a good-sized allotment plot which provides seasonal fruit and vegetables as well as a constant reminder of my own horticultural inadequacy. I keep bees (still very much with 'L' plates) and would go for chickens and even pigs if my space permitted, but sadly it doesn't. I make preserves and wine and store my maincrop vegetables. My garden and allotment are managed to encourage biodiversity, although it would be nice if the foxes and slugs could opt out of this. And as for saving and generating energy, we take many energy- and water-saving measures in the house, but the fact that we plan to move soon means that the investment in a major 'eco-retrofit' is being saved for the next house. Oh, and our (little-used) car runs on vegetable oil.

GROWING YOUR OWN FOOD

Why grow your own food?

It's a very good question. After all, growing food is what farmers are for. Unless we have lots of land and lots of time, why should we bother? Glossy utopian gardening books and self-sufficiency manuals rarely point out the downsides of growing your own food, so let's start by being practical and looking at the pitfalls as well as the pleasures.

Five reasons not to grow your own food

It can cost a lot to get started

In the past, nobody started growing from scratch. Our peasant ancestors inherited everything from their forebears. They didn't really need to buy land or equipment or go on gardening courses: all the kit and the skills they needed were handed down from generation to generation. Today's aspirant grower, hemmed as she or he often is into a small house and garden, usually has a lot of stuff to buy, from garden tools and propagating gear to soil improvers, sheds, water butts – the list is endless.

You won't save much money

In Victorian times, the price of food meant that growing your own would have saved up to 50 per cent of your annual expenditure. Today, we spend only around 10–15 per cent of our income on food and only a fraction of this goes on the stuff you could grow in your garden. If you really want to save money on food and drink, be a teetotal vegetarian.

You will not achieve self-sufficiency in anything other than salads and herbs

Even if we adopt the 'Mediterranean food pyramid' – a diet in which cereals, pulses and vegetables predominate and animal protein forms only a small part – it is very tough to be truly self-sufficient in food, particularly from a small space in a temperate climate. If you give up meat, accept that all your carbohydrates will come from potatoes (which store well and can give bulk yields in small spaces), and brace yourself for lean times and preserved or frozen food in the April–June 'hungry gap', then it's maybe do-able. But desirable? Probably not.

It takes time, particularly when you want to go on holiday

Peasants who learnt to grow as they grew up did not have to invest much time in getting started; and strong social and family networks meant that an equally skilled person was always around to help. Leave your veg garden alone at the wrong time of year, though, and weed apocalypse could greet your return from holiday. Growing food does need an investment of time, often when you least have it.

Children aren't always compatible with horticulture

Few things are more distressing than watching a small child innocently upend a module tray full of carefully tended seedlings. A garden largely given over to growing is not always somewhere in which you can relax with offspring. Compromise is needed to keep parents, kids, fruit and veg happy.

But if you can cope with these downsides, there are of course many, many good reasons for growing your own which far outweigh the disadvantages.

Five reasons to grow your own food

It is deeply satisfying . . .

Even if it's just the one radish that escaped the slugs, the satisfaction of eating your own produce is enormous and hard to communicate to those who haven't given it a go. And the more time and effort you invest in raising a particular plant, the better it feels when you finally eat its produce. Knowing how much effort it can take to get, say, a humble sprouting broccoli plant from seed to plate (propagating, transplanting, protecting – over maybe ten months) also gives a deep appreciation of the value of food.

. . . and very healthy

More is being discovered all the time about the true nutritional value of food. And the evidence suggests that modern, industrial agricultural techniques not only damage the land and expose us to pesticides and herbicides: they have also depleted both the mineral and micronutrient content of vegetables and fruit in the last fifty or so years. Buying seasonal, local organic food helps avoid this; but growing your own gives you total control over what goes into your food. The nutrient content of fruit and vegetables is optimal when they have just been picked. Plus, of course, you get to spend time exercising in the fresh air.

You will have new gourmet experiences

We are accustomed to buying food, refrigerating it and then eating it when we're ready. And if it's from a supermarket, it has already spent far too much time on the road and in a fridge. For many vegetables and fruit, this does terrible things to their nutritional value and to their gourmet appeal. The garden, however, keeps fruit and veg in perfect condition, so if you get into the habit of picking and eating straight away, the quality is streets ahead of anything you could buy in the shops. For particular produce – herbs, salads, tomatoes, soft fruit (see pp. 24–7 for a table with a 'gourmet value' rating) – this is absolutely crucial.

You can stick two fingers up at the modern food industry

Every time I pick a sprig of thyme from the garden I think of over-packaged herbs grown in a monster high-tech greenhouse somewhere and sold for a ludicrous price by supermarkets. And I rejoice in the small victory of depriving these undeserving behemoths of a tiny bit of revenue. If you hate the modern food chain and what it's doing to the land and to communities, then growing your own is a small, maybe insignificant, but satisfying political act.

You will learn a great deal and develop new skills

In learning to grow food, you inevitably find out a great deal of fascinating stuff about nature, from soil composition to the role of flora and fauna to weather and seasons. This is satisfying in itself; and it also brings you closer to the seasons and the cycle of life in a way that introduces constant variety and interest into your life. And of course you learn a whole range of skills – composting, planting, amateur weather forecasting – that enrich your life and can be passed on to others.

What are vegetables and fruit?

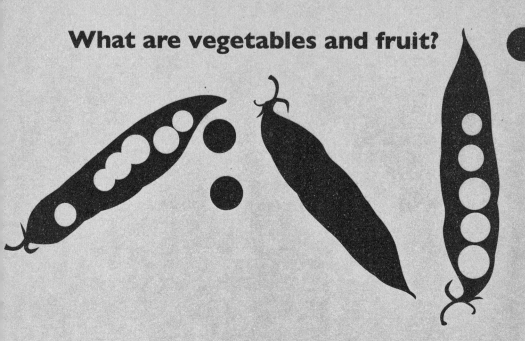

Before I started growing fruit and vegetables I knew very little about how, why and when they grew. And I found that many gardening books seemed to skip this fundamental information and dive straight into gardening techniques and principles.

If, as I was (and still feel!), you are a complete newcomer to edible gardening, then I think it's worth going right back to first principles and taking a quick look at what fruit and vegetables are, and how they behave through the year. It's not essential to help you plan your time: but it's useful and perhaps interesting background.

Most of the vegetables that we grow are 'annuals', which means that the plants die off every year, having put all their energy into setting (producing) seed. We eat this energy (which is contained in different parts of these vegetables) at different points in their seed-setting cycles, depending on what's best. So with 'leaf vegetables', like lettuce and cabbages, we eat the leaves because these are good and the seeds are tiny. (However, rapeseed oil – made from the seeds of a cabbage relative – forms a huge part of the modern food chain.) With peas and beans we eat the immature seeds. Sometimes we eat the unopened flowers (as in broccoli); or the stems (celery); or the root (parsnip, carrot). And sometimes we eat the 'fruit' that contains the seeds, as with tomatoes, cucumber or pumpkins.

Temperature and day length are the main factors that affect when things grow. Below 6°C, plants are dormant and nothing grows: so in the depths of winter in Britain the growing season grinds to a halt. (Global warming is, however, rapidly bringing a year-round growing season to much of Britain.) Increasing day length from January onwards kicks off the growth of a small number of plants (such as rhubarb) that respond to this. And then increasing warmth prompts more natural growth and eventually heats the soil enough for planting many things outside. By May, weeds are in aggressive competition with your young vegetables. The first, early outdoor crops are ready by May and June, and then, as the summer warms up, more and more produce becomes available. By August and September, peak harvest season, sowing and planting activity starts to tail off, and into the autumn the business of preparing the soil for the next year's growing season starts up.

Over the centuries we have selectively bred different types of vegetables – and taken advantage of their different characteristics – to provide us, as much as possible, with a year-round supply within the constraints of our temperate, four-season climate.

Root vegetables such as carrots, parsnips, swede and turnips store goodness in their roots over the winter to power a vibrant flowering in the spring. We take advantage of this concentrated nutrition, either lifting and storing the roots when they are ready or leaving them in the ground until we want to eat them. The same principle applies to leaf vegetables: we take the energy stored in their leaves before they flower and turn it to seed. For fast-growing salads, this means a quick meal, early on in the growing season. And for hardy, slow-growing winter cabbages, it means fresh greens in the coldest months. Pea and bean plants, well-adapted to our climate, flower and set seed early in the growing season, enabling us to eat their immature seeds in the early summer; whilst non-native 'fruiting' vegetables like tomatoes need more heat and light to come to fruition.

Fruit, on the other hand, is perennial, growing on trees and shrubs over many years, depending on the species. So because fruit has to complete a cycle of growth, flowering and fruiting before it's ready to eat, it tends to have a short season, during – and mostly towards the end of – the warmest months in our climate (unless we cheat nature with greenhouses and heating).

There are also perennial vegetables, which present the edible gardener with a low-effort (if sometimes space-intensive) food-growing option. Artichokes, asparagus, sorrel and rhubarb (botanically a vegetable) are just three examples of plants which, once established, will continue cropping in their seasons with minimal intervention from the gardener.

It's not essential to know all this background in order to plan your edible gardening time. But it's helpful. If, for example, you have very little time to spare through the year and spend lots of time away, then the best strategy would be to concentrate on fruit trees and bushes and perennial vegetables. Such a food-growing operation can take a long time to establish itself (the trees have to grow and mature) and its yields are lower and concentrated more on fruit. But there's much less need to worry about maintenance and, crucially, no need for sowing, propagating and planting once it's established.

Grow annual vegetables and you will need more time, depending on what you want to eat. A simple balcony-based salads and herbs operation won't take much time at all. But growing annuals to get a constant year-round supply of fresh food does take a little more effort; and there are times when it's good not to go away.

The 21st-Century Smallholder's Year Planner (pp. 144–157) gives a full run-down of the edible gardening year and the time taken by other related things – such as beekeeping or pond-building – that you may or may not wish to explore. Read through this and you will quickly build up a picture of when different things happen, and which are the busiest and quietest months.

The table below summarizes in brief how the growing year pans out. In reality, many of these tasks go on all the time. But this gives a picture of how the intensity of work needed follows the growing season.

SOWING, PLANTING AND HARVESTING

	J	F	M	A	M	J	J	A	S	O	N	D
Soil preparation	▥	▥									▥	▥
Sowing/planting		▯	▥	▥	▥	▥	▥	▯	|	|	|	|
Propagating		▥	▥	▥								
Weeding		|	▯	▥	▥	▥	▥	▥	▯	|	|	|
Harvesting	|	|	|	▯	▥	▥	▥	▥	▥	▥	▯	|
Watering						▥	▥	|				
Days per month*	1	1	1	2	2	2	2	2	2	2	1	1

* Very rough estimate for a large vegetable plot of, say, 100 square metres.

▥ = lots of work needed ▯ = little work needed

Where to start?

Fruit- and veg-growing often seems like a huge and daunting subject and it is the subject of many huge and daunting books. Perhaps the easiest way to start is to consider your space. Do you have a window box, a balcony, a small garden or a big garden? Or maybe an allotment too? Does it get lots of sun? Lots of wind? Lots of rain? What's the soil like? Is there any? Even if it's just a window box, you'll be able to grow things all year round; but the size and nature of your space will help determine what to grow.

Then there's the question of what you want to eat. Perhaps it's things like tomatoes and strawberries that never taste as good as when picked and eaten straight off the plant. Or maybe you're after maximum yield, for example growing potatoes in a tub to get a huge supply from just a few square feet.

Finally there's the question of your time. How much do you have? Will it be a snatched fifteen minutes every evening, or an afternoon a week? Or more? And on the subject of time, how long can you wait? Six weeks for some salads to grow, or six years for a 'forest garden' to start establishing itself?

There are, of course, other variables to worry about: how much hassle a particular plant is to grow, how long its season is, how good it looks . . . but space, time and what you want to eat will help you to make some practical choices to get started.

The table on pp. 24–7 'scores' fruit and veg according to these factors: browsing through it will give you an idea of what things will suit you and help you to decide where to start with growing your own food.

Vegetable		Comments
Artichoke, globe		Easy to grow (it's a thistle), tastes great, looks good too, but each plant takes up a great deal of space.
Artichoke, Jerusalem		Very space-hungry but highly nutritious and a good crop for breaking up the ground.
Asparagus		Needs permanent, dedicated space and lots of time to mature. But perennial and with unmatched gourmet value.
Aubergine		Needs greenhouse, preferably heated. Not a natural for the British climate.
Beans, broad		Tough plant, easy to grow, great gourmet value, provides different delicacies throughout its season (pods, fresh beans, dried beans).
Beans, French		Slightly more finicky than broad beans, but great gourmet value and yield.
Beans, runner		A garden favourite, but there are things that taste better . . .
Beetroot		Easy to grow and can be eaten at various stages; also stores well.
Broccoli, Calabrese		The nutritional value of your own broccoli is (just about) worth the hassle of growing it.
Broccoli, sprouting		Space-hungry and with a long growing season, but provides a superb delicacy in late winter when little else is fresh.
Brussels sprouts		Need a lot of room, but taste great and stand through the winter.
Cabbage		The huge variety of cabbages can provide fresh veg all year round, but plants can be space-hungry.
Cardoon		A gourmet treat, but only for those with room to spare.
Carrots		Can be tricky to grow and prefer lighter soils.

Key: Space Time Gourmet 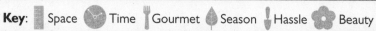 Season Hassle Beauty

Cauliflower			Pest-prone like all brassicas and needs a lot of water. Long growing season.
Celeriac			Long growing season and hard to produce a big bulb.
Celery			'Trench' celery is hard work, self-blanching type is easier.
Chard			Easy to grow, looks lovely, tastes great and stands through the winter.
Chicory			Complex range of varieties; can be labour-intensive but fine eating.
Courgettes			Take up some space but very easy to grow and crops heavily.
Cucumber			Ideally needs to be grown in a greenhouse or polytunnel.
Endive			The taste of chicory without the hassle. A good year-round, small-space crop.
Fennel			Works best in warm areas.
Garlic			Hardy, space-efficient and very healthy.
Kale			A great standby through the winter: hardy and easy to grow.
Kohlrabi			Beautiful, tasty, not demanding of space and can be grown nearly all year round.
Leeks			A 21st-Century Smallholder's essential. Lots of tasty produce through the winter from small space.
Lettuce			Everyone should grow it: a cold frame or greenhouse extends the season nearly all year round.
Onions			Store well and give a good yield for the space they occupy.
Onions, spring			Tasty, handy and useful for small spaces.

Key: ■ 4 (excellent) ■ 3 ■ 2 ■ 1 (not so good)

Parsnips		Very long growing season. Needs same conditions as carrots. Magnet for insects if left to flower.
Peas		Nothing beats your own peas. Don't take up too much space but do need support. Also add to soil fertility.
Peppers and chillies		A greenhouse or windowsill proposition.
Potatoes		Vast yield available from small spaces; great tastes, too.
Radishes		Fast growing and fiery-flavoured: a salad essential.
Rhubarb		Needs its own (large) space but looks after itself once established.
Rocket		Easy and quick to grow, tastes great, an edible gardening must.
Sorrel		Perennial, hassle-free and one of the first interesting flavours of the growing year.
Spinach		Easy to grow, versatile, long season.
Squash (winter) and pumpkins		Needs space but can be 'trailed' between other plants. Great late summer/autumn treat and can store well.
Swede		Slow growing, likes cool conditions, a good winter standby.
Sweetcorn		Needs a good summer, but worth it for the unparalleled gourmet experience.
Tomatoes		Easy to grow but need feeding and watering, especially if in containers. Gourmet value makes it all worthwhile.
Turnips		Very tasty and the leaves can be eaten too. Reasonably space-efficient.

Key: Space Time Gourmet  Season Hassle Beauty

Fruit		Comments
Apple and crabapple		Obviously not a window-box proposition, but worth it for delightful blossom and the endless
Blackberry		Vigorous is an understatement: they'll have your whole garden given a chance.
Blackcurrant		Needs netting but tastes great and fruit is hugely nutritious. Plants not too big.
Blueberry		Tremendously good for you. But needs acid soil.
Cherry		Different types can fit into different parts of the garden.
Elderberry		Abundant in the wild, but why not have your own supply?
Gooseberry		Hardy, easy to grow and a superb seasonal treat.
Medlar		Almost impossible to find this quirky fruit in the shops; trees are beautiful too.
Mulberry		Superb summer treat, unobtainable commercially. Takes a long time to crop.
Pear		Not as hardy as apples, but still beautiful and tasty.
Plum (and relatives)		Essential summer fruit. Plums don't like cooler springs but damsons grow well further north.
Quince		Very attractive tree and unusual fruit.
Raspberry		An essential fruit for the edible garden.
Red and white currants		Good for jellies and summer pudding.
Strawberry		Nothing tastes better than your own.

Key: 4 (excellent) 3 2 1 (not so good)

How are you going to garden?

Another important starting point is to decide how you are going to garden. If you are planning to do things organically, then you will need less money – because there is no need to buy pesticides, herbicides and artificial fertilizer – but more time, because, for example, you will need to do more weeding and crop protection.

Conventional

Applied to cultivation, this term somewhat ironically refers to the less than sixty-year-old technique of growing food crops with a reliance on 'scientific' intervention: artificial fertilizers, pesticides and herbicides. It's an adversarial way of tackling the land: man vs. nature. Growing food this way may bring quick results, but its downsides are numerous. It will cost more in the short term, because the inputs you need are expensive; and it will cost more in the long term, because growing food this way depletes biodiversity, puts toxic substances into the food chain and exhausts your soil. To find out more about conventional growing, buy a different book!

Organic

Going organic means growing food with an absolute minimum of scientific intervention and with a focus on improving the soil. It is ideally suited to the 21st-Century Smallholder's edible gardening efforts because it's cheap, makes your garden more fertile over time and encourages a biodiversity that helps to protect what you grow as well as making your garden beautiful. Rather than fighting nature, organic growing seeks to recruit natural predators to deal with pests, uses natural barriers such as mulches to deal with weeds and natural fertilizers like home-made compost to enrich the soil. 'Biodynamic' growing adds further techniques to organic principles, using an astronomical calendar to determine auspicious planting times and treating compost with special herbs.

Permaculture

Edible gardening according to permaculture principles means working organically, but taking natural ecosystems as a model for what you do. So the ultimate permaculture food-growing operation is a managed 'forest garden' in which the careful choice and siting of trees and mainly perennial plants provides an ultra low-maintenance, sustainable food source. This can be hard to achieve in practice, particularly in temperate climates. However, the permaculture principles of careful planning and of maximizing the beneficial relationships between people, plants and animals are very useful, particularly when gardening in small spaces.

The recommended ways of growing in this book are based on a combination of organic and permaculture principles.

Planning your space

The next step is to plan your growing space. It is enormously tempting to get carried away and see the entire garden or outside space as nothing more than a food-growing operation – after all, there's so much good stuff to grow! However, the obvious pitfall of this is that the garden ceases to be a space for leisure, or even for biodiversity. Children and a gardening-enthusiast wife soon made me realize that our meagre outside space needed to be more than just a mini market garden. And organic gardening dictates that there should be some space for wildlife habitats, including maybe a pond to encourage slug-eating frogs, as well as room for a decent compost heap and a rainwater butt. (See also Chapter 4 for more on building biodiversity.)

Answering the following set of questions will help you to plan your food-growing operation.

What do I want to do with my outside space? If it's going to be used exclusively for food-growing, then fine: but bear in mind that, in gardening organically, you will need room for plants and features that encourage pest predators; crops will need to be rotated (see pp. 55–6) and you will benefit hugely from a compost heap, rainwater collection and even a small greenhouse. Most of us will want our garden or outside space to be several things: a playground for the kids, somewhere to eat, a wildlife haven, a retreat – maybe all of these. The sample 21st-Century Smallholder's garden designs on pp. 32–41 are based on a balance between food-growing, leisure and creating the biodiversity that is essential to organic gardening (and also fascinating for children and adults alike).

How big is it? Size matters when it comes to edible gardening. There's little point, for example, in growing space-hungry Brussels sprouts on a balcony. You can produce an awful lot in a small space (see example on p. 33), but choosing space-efficient plants and trees is the most sensible way to do it. (It is surprising how many different fruit and vegetables are appropriate for small spaces – see table on pp. 24–7.) As your space gets bigger, you have more room for luxuries like greenhouses, chickens, bigger ponds; and the choice of vegetables you can grow widens to include really space-hungry gourmet crops like asparagus and artichokes.

What's there already? If it's all paved or decked then you have work to do: but this could involve using containers or building raised beds (see pp. 46–7) rather than digging the whole lot up. There's maybe stuff you could use: trees and shrubs that provide great wildlife habitat, for example. And you'll also have to consider the soil (see pp. 42–5), which will probably need some form of improvement to support greedy fruit and vegetables.

Which way does it point? North or south, up or down? Orientation is another factor to consider. Tomatoes would delight in a south-facing wall; a small morello cherry tree won't mind the shade. If it's steep, some terracing might be necessary to create viable vegetable beds.

What's the climate like? Whether you live in Bristol or Braemar will affect the things you can grow. Latitude and elevation will determine, for example, whether certain fruit trees really are viable; or whether you'll get a decent crop of sweetcorn. 'Microclimate' should also be considered: if you have, say, particularly windy, wet, sunny, shady or frost-prone spots, these should all be taken into account when planning your food-growing.

The 'Meet the fruit and veg' section on pp. 64–95 will help you to decide which plants will work in your outside space. And the three sample designs which follow will illustrate how these can integrate into an outside space that provides for food, leisure and wildlife, whether it's a small balcony, average-sized garden or large garden.

Three garden designs

The balcony

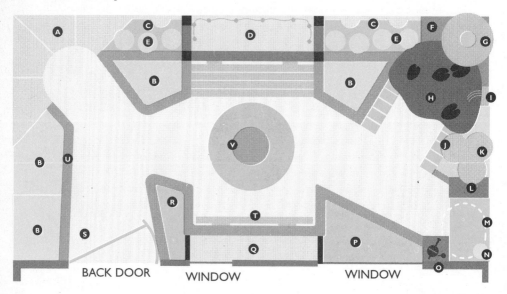

BACK DOOR   WINDOW   WINDOW

A   Greenhouse for toms/cucumbers and all-year cropping of salads etc.
B   Annual rotational veg beds
C   Fruit tree against wall
D   Head board and small (40cm) covered trellis and pagoda for vines & soft fruit
E   Summer salads
F   'Wild' area under tree
G   Standard fruit tree
H   Raised pond
I   Fountain
J   Raised brick seat
K   Permanent bed (rhubarb etc.)
L   Compost bin, against the wall
M   Storage shed

N   Filter-in downpipe to underground water tank
O   Watering can fed by hand pump bringing water up from the tank
P   Permanent bed (strawberries and asparagus)
Q   Raised 'head board' bed for herbs & flowers
R   Herbs at ground level (20cm)
S   Permanent reclaimed brick path
T   Bench
U   'New' sleeper edging
V   Solid table with permanent central herb buffet!

1. The balcony

Lack of a garden needn't stop you being a 21st-Century Smallholder. You may not get vast yields from tiny spaces but, as this illustration shows, even a small balcony can provide a huge amount of variety for the committed flat-dweller. This design ticks all the boxes: it is a space for leisure, food-growing and biodiversity, all crammed into a mere 4m x 2m (13ft x 6.5ft).

In this example, as in many of our homes, the orientation isn't perfect: the balcony faces east and slightly to the north, so this has influenced where things go. On a south-facing balcony, the back wall would be the obvious place to put plants that love heat and sun. Here, the growing activity is arranged so that different plants get maximum benefit from the balcony's orientation. On the north (left) side, two half-metre-wide beds (raised about 40cm from the ground) will expose annual vegetables to the best light; and next to these, a small customized greenhouse will provide excellent summer crops of tomatoes and cucumbers as well as a year-round supply of small salad plants and leaves. A third bed to the right of the greenhouse provides more space for annual vegetables. Behind this is a small salad bed. As we move round the design clockwise we come to the centrepiece: two folding benches and a table at whose centre is a living herb 'buffet'. Behind one of the benches there is room for vines and soft fruit to grow up and over a small trellis and pagoda. To the right of this is room for more salads and a fourth annual vegetable bed – even in such a small space, there is room for the classic crop rotation of organic cultivation (see pp. 55–6 for more on crop rotation).

The south-east (top right) corner of this balcony is a riot of activity. There's a tiny wilderness area underneath a small fruit tree. A raised pond with a fountain will provide beauty, relaxation and a haven for all manner of beneficial bugs and creatures. Small seats next to the pond provide a restful spot in your own 'wild' space.

As we move into the shadier part of the design, permanent beds for rhubarb, asparagus and strawberries flank a small compost bin and shed: and for those with a ground-floor balcony and the appropriate permission, there's space here for an underground water butt too. Behind the east-facing bench on the back wall, there's a raised bed for herbs and flowers; and another herb bed right by the back door, where you need it.

2. The average garden

It's not easy to get a fix on how big the 'average' garden in Britain is. Research from a major DIY chain suggests as much as 300 square metres, which at around 30 by 100 feet (in old money) is a pretty big space. A Royal Horticultural Society/Wildlife Trusts survey reckons that there are fifteen million gardens in Britain covering 270,000 hectares, which makes the average a more modest 180 square metres. But this still seems a lot for the houses in which most of us live today and is probably skewed by a few very big gardens. So based on some more sources and a bit of educated guesswork, I've chosen 100 square metres as an area to represent what those of us who live in houses or garden flats are most likely to have available.

Obviously, every space is different in terms of shape, orientation, climate and what's there already. But whatever it's like, unless your garden has really extreme environmental constraints – far too much shade, a very severe slope – there's a lot you can do with it. And most constraints can be dealt with: terracing to deal with slopes, sheltering barriers to deal with wind.

This 'average' garden measures 12.5m x 7.5m (41ft x 25ft) and faces east (which is not ideal: south-facing is best). It illustrates how a still-modest space can be productive, diverse, beautiful and practical. The pathways and area nearest the house are all paved (perhaps with old bricks) for ease of maintenance and to control weeds. Gravel or mulched paths might not be as sturdy and grass pathways would be prone to muddiness and impossible to mow. Nearest the house is all the stuff to which you need easy access: a lean-to store for garden kit, a pump from an underground rainwater tank (which, at maybe 1,000-litre capacity, will be all the irrigation water you will ever need), a window box of herbs and a dining area, sheltered with an edible canopy of vines.

Then there's a children's play area and flower/veg bed for them to experiment with, and a flower-bordered lawn with a fruit tree. The vegetable-growing operation starts in earnest about halfway down the garden, with four beds to accommodate the traditional rotation of annual vegetables, for example legumes (peas and beans), brassicas (cabbages, kale), alliums (onions, leeks) and potatoes. There are also permanent beds for useful gourmet perennials like rhubarb, artichoke and asparagus. Using the available space to the maximum – whilst at the same time creating natural beauty – fruit trees are trained along the south-facing wall and also over arches that form a 'living walkway' between the vegetable beds.

At the bottom of the garden is a lot of practical stuff that also provides another relaxing haven. The greenhouse will take care of all the seed trays and potting activity in the spring and summer whilst providing a supply of fresh salads through the autumn and winter. A bench provides a restful spot in a small, fragrant niche of herbs. And then, slightly concealed by a fruit tree, are the compost bins and comfrey patch that are an essential feature of any organic garden. Next to that, shaded by the north-facing wall, is a chicken house and fenced-off run, with room for two hens (giving you a supply of 200–600 eggs per year, depending on breed). The hens also get access to a small 'orchard' of cobnut and hazel bushes. This is permanently enclosed on the north side by a fence along which soft fruit like raspberries can be trained; and in the middle, a fence of wattle hurdles allows the chickens to be 'rotated' on each side of the orchard to avoid too much damage to the ground and to prevent the build-up of parasites. Alternatively, the chickens' space could be occupied by beehives and the ground in the orchard left to develop as a small wildflower meadow around the bushes.

The pond, which will play host to pest predators such as frogs as well as being decorative, is bordered with fences and a bench to discourage small children, but also has a shallow 'beach' area to help its amphibious inhabitants get in and out. And to the south and west of the pond is a wild space of long grass and native hedging which will provide food and habitat for insects and birds.

So this garden will provide the 21st-Century Smallholder with a great deal in the way of food, leisure, beauty and biodiversity. Such an area won't make you self-sufficient in vegetables – far from it – but, carefully managed, it will provide fresh, local vegetables and herbs all year round, a good supply of fruit in season, fresh eggs or more honey than you need. Despite the compost heaps, you will probably need to import fertility in the form of compost or manure, but with a bed system (see pp. 46–7) this can simply be applied to the surface rather than dug in, for a low-effort, 'no-dig' approach to gardening. The eating and relaxation spaces, the lawn and the pond make sure that the space is a haven and not just a market garden; and the wilderness areas will encourage wildlife that the children will enjoy and the crop predators will fear.

Such a garden won't be expensive. With the exception, perhaps, of the proposed bridge over the pond, much of the structural stuff can be DIY: compost bins, fencing, raised beds, even the chicken-house. The pond can be built easily using a butyl liner (see p. 139). The most expensive items are likely to be the greenhouse and the purchase of the fruit trees: but these are investments that pay back dividends over a long time.

The average garden

A Greenhouse against wall 1.5m x 2.25m
B Potting bench
C Raised herb bed and planter
D Bench
E Herbs
F Comfrey bed
G Compost bins
H Fruit tree
I Cosy 2 x chicken house
J Soft fruit along fence
K Fenced chicken run
L Cobnut and hazel bushes
M Wattle hurdles
N Raised brick asparagus beds
O Wooden bridge over the pond
P Wild space
Q Flow form fountain
R Native hedge
S Paved pathway
T Hand-pump water from tank
U Lean-to storage shed (forks, spades etc)
V Wall-trained fruit trees
W Underground water storage tank
X Downpipe with in-line filter
Y Vine-covered seating
Z Bark chips
0 Sand pit
2 Wendy house
3 Kids' garden veg etc.
4 Annual rotational veg beds
5 Trained fruit arches/tunnels
6 Shallow 'beach' area
7 Flower bed
8 Permanent bed
9 Solid bench

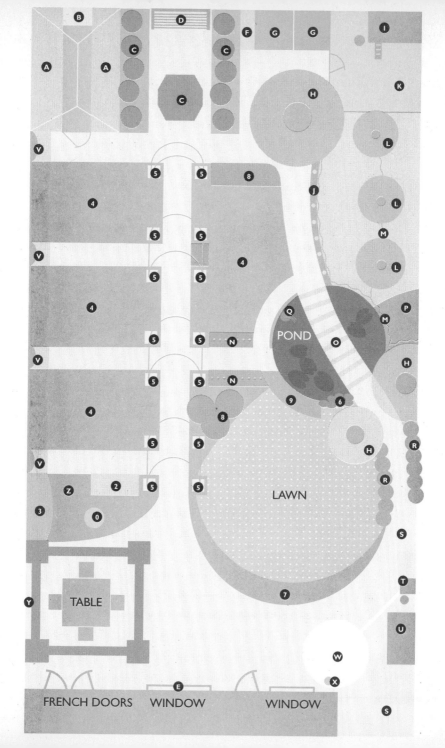

POND

LAWN

TABLE

FRENCH DOORS   WINDOW   WINDOW

3. The substantial space

For those blessed with big gardens, 21st-Century Smallholding options expand yet further. This example measures approximately 300 square metres: it's about 23m (74ft) from the back of the house to the end of the garden and about 19m (62ft) across at the widest point. This may be big, but it's still only 0.07 of an acre (0.03 hectares) and it's amazing just how much activity can happen in a space that is still a great deal smaller than a real smallholding.

As with all these examples, the orientation isn't perfect: this is a north-facing garden so space has to be left to allow for the shade cast by the house on the food-growing operation. This design has plenty of space for leisure: a kids' garden, a generous seating area and a lawn; as well as plenty of growing space. The four rotational vegetable beds of 1.2m x 5m (4ft x 16ft) will provide a large supply of annual vegetables through the year; and two-and-a-half permanent beds will provide low-maintenance gourmet perennial crops like rhubarb, asparagus, artichokes and strawberries. All the beds are arranged north–south to minimize shading, and flower beds at the south end of each one provide interest and attract insects. A lavender and herb 'walk' between the two groups of beds will provide scent, flavouring and another reason for beneficial insects to visit.

Like all these designs, this garden uses the permaculture principle of 'zoning', in which things are placed not only according to orientation and microclimate but also according to how much attention they need and how much use they get. So herbs, salads, the greenhouse and annual vegetables are near the house, making it easy to nip out and pick something (or shortening the trip for a night-time slug hunt). The orchard, undersown with a wildflower meadow, needs much less maintenance and is therefore further away. OK, so the chickens and compost bins will need daily visits, but it's hardly an onerous walk. Six full-sized fruit trees will give you a serious crop of fine seasonal fruit; and the orchard also doubles as a chicken run for up to eight birds, who can be rotated on either side of a central fence to make sure they don't damage the ground and always have a good surface to scratch on. In a garden this size, there's ample space for a couple of beehives too, which in a good year will provide far more honey than a family could eat.

On the east (right-hand) side of the garden are some small cobnut trees, providing another seasonal crop as long as you can get to them before the squirrels do. And there's a pond for wildlife and aesthetic interest: in this example it has a solar-powered fountain. Next to this is another benefit of the large garden: a permanently covered soft-fruit cage. Netting fruits such as blackcurrants, raspberries and gooseberries is labour-intensive and having a permanent cage gets rid of the bird problem for good.

A friend of mine once said, 'You can never have too many sheds.' There will be a lot of paraphernalia associated with a garden like this, from hand tools to beekeeping gear and chicken feed. There's only one shed here, but it's big: and it doubles as a space for growing soft fruit.

Finally, to the west (left) of the house, there's space for a good-sized greenhouse, which can be used for raising and potting seedlings as well as growing heat-loving summer crops and keeping a winter supply of salads going. Just next to this, the wall space behind the herb and salads beds is used for 'trained' fruit trees.

The substantial space

A Chicken house for 8 chickens
& rotational runs
B Wild-flower meadow
C Beehives
D Bench
E Herbs
F Cobnuts
G Compost bins
H Fruit trees
I Comfrey beds
J Covered soft-fruit cage
K Greenhouse
L Pond and fountain fed by batteries and
solar panel on fruit cage
M Solar panel
N Permanent beds for asparagus,
strawberries, rhubarb, Jerusalem
and globe artichokes etc.
O Kids' garden

P Wall garden for herbs
Q Annual rotational veg beds
R Native hedge
S Paved pathway
T Thyme and marjoram in cracks
of the walk
U Soft fruit over door
V Flower beds
W Pump
X Downpipe with in-line filter
Y Seating
Z Salads
2 Wendy house

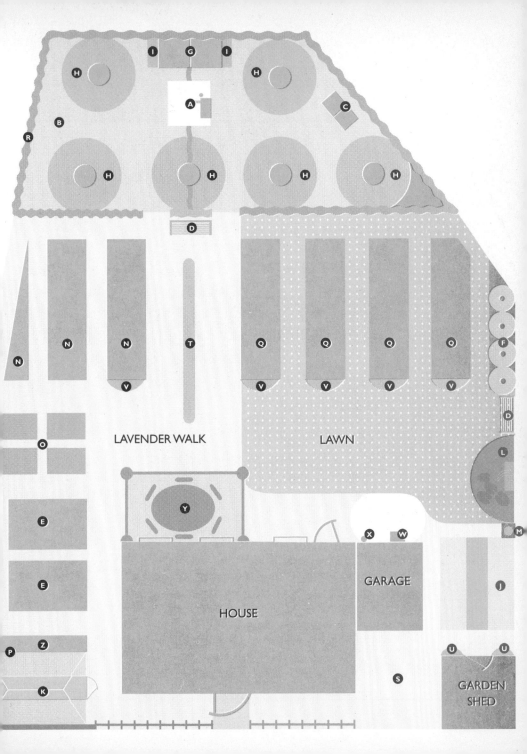

Preparing and managing the ground

'You are what you eat' is a maxim that applies to fruit and vegetables as well as people. If plants eat 'junk food' like artificial fertilizer, then they may grow fast but won't necessarily contain the good stuff that makes them worth eating in the first place. 'Chemical' agriculture depletes the soil, rather than building its fertility. This is supported not only by evidence in the 'developed' world of topsoil loss and erosion but also by studies which show sharp declines in the mineral and micronutrient content of vegetables since the advent of industrial farming. Growing your own food gives you total control over (at least part of) your diet. And it all starts with the soil, a gramme of which can contain more than a billion organisms of ten thousand species. Plants take up nutrients from the soil and pass them on to us when we eat them: our job as edible gardeners is to make sure we replace and build this fertility so the soil, the plants and those who eat them stay healthy. So the ultimate aim of a 21st-Century Smallholder who wants to get healthy plants is to build good soil.

Clearing the ground

If you are lucky and have bare soil all ready for planting, then you won't have to worry about this first step. But for many of us, starting out with growing fruit and veg involves clearing away what's there already. Once you've got rid of major obstructions like paving slabs or unwanted trees and roots, there are a couple of ways of doing this:

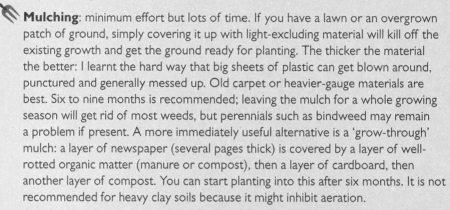

Mulching: minimum effort but lots of time. If you have a lawn or an overgrown patch of ground, simply covering it up with light-excluding material will kill off the existing growth and get the ground ready for planting. The thicker the material the better: I learnt the hard way that big sheets of plastic can get blown around, punctured and generally messed up. Old carpet or heavier-gauge materials are best. Six to nine months is recommended; leaving the mulch for a whole growing season will get rid of most weeds, but perennials such as bindweed may remain a problem if present. A more immediately useful alternative is a 'grow-through' mulch: a layer of newspaper (several pages thick) is covered by a layer of well-rotted organic matter (manure or compost), then a layer of cardboard, then another layer of compost. You can start planting into this after six months. It is not recommended for heavy clay soils because it might inhibit aeration.

Digging or rotovating: hard work but much quicker. If you want to get going straight away, then more effort is called for. Digging will loosen up the soil and enable you to incorporate organic material into it. It does not, however, have to be an ongoing, onerous part of the gardening year: in many cases, once the ground is dug, you need never do it again (see 'To dig or not to dig' on p. 45). Soil in new housing developments or that has been uncovered beneath paving may well be compacted and denuded of fertility, so digging will be essential to aerate and 'open up' the soil as well as to incorporate organic matter. A rotovator will make faster work of larger areas. 'Double digging' may be necessary if the subsoil is deeply compacted: it involves digging sections of ground to two spades' depth (turning over both topsoil and subsoil) and incorporating organic matter as you go. Turf can also be 'dug in' in this way, if an area of grassland or lawn is being cleared: it needs to be buried at the subsoil level (to stop it re-growing) in a practice delightfully known as 'bastard trenching'.

Testing the soil

Clay or sand? Acid or alkali? It's worth checking before you start sowing. Very sandy soils are easy to work but drain quickly, so need lots of organic matter adding to them, whilst at the other end of the scale, soils with a lot of clay hold moisture and fertility well but can be heavy and hard to work (see 'Improvement strategies') on p. 44. At my London allotment, the heavy clay soil is rock-hard in summer and a gluey bog in winter: choosing the right time to work it is vital. The quick and easy way to check your soil type is to pick some up, moisten it and try to roll it into a ball. If it won't cohere at all, it's probably sand; if it forms a gritty ball it's loam; and if it forms a sticky ball, it's likely to be clay or silt.

As to the pH, this determines what will thrive. As a rule, the wetter the local climate in this country, the more acid the soil is likely to be. The ideal is a neutral pH of 6–7, which suits most things. You may, however, want to create a soil 'microclimate' for acid-loving edible plants such as blueberries: containers (see pp. 46–7) are one way of doing this. Soil-testing kits are cheap and easily available from garden equipment retailers.

Improvement strategies

To get soil in the best shape for edible gardening, it needs a good structure and a balance of the major elements – nitrogen, phosphorous and potassium (often referred to as NPK) – that plants need. Artificial fertilizers will provide a 'fix' of these but won't build soil fertility. The best materials to add are:

Compost: garden compost (see p. 48) is an excellent all-round source of fertility and improves soil structure. However, if you're just starting out, your own home-made stuff is unlikely to be ready for a while. You can buy in compost cheaply from some local authorities; and, of course, there's a huge range of commercial compost available. Be sure to avoid anything containing peat: it's good stuff, but comes from an unsustainable source. 'Eco-friendly' compost can be found at good garden centres and from mail-order suppliers.

Manure: horse, cow and pig manure are great sources of nitrogen. Most of the goodness comes from the straw, which contains the animals' urine and also conditions the soil. It is essential that manure is well rotted, or composted over several months, to stabilize the nutrients in it. Farms and stables are the best sources of manure: buying it in bags from garden centres is ruinously expensive as I discovered when two tiny veg beds effortlessly swallowed up fifty quid's worth of bagged manure.

Leafmould: (see p. 50) won't add much in the way of fertility but is very good for improving the structure of hard-to-work soils like clay.

Strategies for different soils

In organic gardening, soil fertility is also maintained by rotating crops (see p. 55) and by using 'green manures' (see p. 56). These can be particularly useful in smaller spaces as a way of keeping bare ground covered during the autumn and winter. When the crop is mature it can simply be hoed off and left as a mulch, where the worms will do the hard work of incorporating it into the soil. Nitrogen-fixing legumes (such as field beans or winter tares) and grasses such as grazing rye are the most common green manures.

STRATEGIES FOR DIFFERENT SOILS	
Clay	Dig in grit, fork in or mulch with well-rotted manure or compost, leafmould.
Sand	Add copious organic matter and mulch with regular quantities of it.
Acid soils	Add ground lime (but not at the same time as manure – leave a few months after liming before manuring).
Alkaline soils	Add compost and manure.

The traditional image of vegetable gardening is of an annual cycle which involves regular, laborious digging. However, once the soil is prepared it is not always necessary to submit yourself to this drudgery, which can harm the soil as well as your back. As long as your soil is in reasonable shape and not compacted, it is possible simply to keep adding a mulch of well-rotted organic matter to the surface and to let the worms do the digging for you. As well as being hard work, digging can damage soil structure and bring weed seeds to the surface so they can germinate. An essential tenet of 'no-dig' gardening is not to tread on the soil, so it is particularly appropriate for bed systems and raised beds (see pp. 46–7).

To dig or not to dig?

DIGGING	NO DIGGING
Advantages	**Advantages**
Breaks up compacted soil	Reduces the loss of water and organic matter
Exposes soil pests to predators and cold weather	Preserves and enhances soil structure
Kills annual weeds	Encourages earthworms, microbes and mycorrhizzas
	Takes minimum effort
	Doesn't bring weed seeds to the surface
Disadvantages	**Disadvantages**
Increases loss of moisture and organic matter	Can take longer to improve soil
Reduces earthworm, microbe and mycorrhizza populations	Doesn't expose soil pests to predators and cold
Adversely affects soil structure	Only appropriate for very heavy soils once they have been thoroughly improved
Brings weed seeds to the surface	
Takes lots of hard work *	

* Some may, however, see this as an advantage: my late friend Helen Stuffins (to whom this book is dedicated) was a highly accomplished organic allotment gardener and confessed to enjoying 'just mindless digging' more than almost any other task on her plot.

Beds and containers

Go to any allotment site and you will see 'row cropping' – the traditional veg-growing practice of cultivating the entire area of the plot, leaving spaces between rows of plants for access to the plants for watering, weeding and harvesting. This technique maximizes use of the space available but inevitably results in some soil compaction, which increases the need for digging.

Far better suited to low-effort, organic vegetable gardening in small spaces is a bed system. If vegetables are grown in narrow beds, the soil need never be trodden on, meaning that, once it is in good shape, it need never be dug and its structure and fertility can improve gradually over time. Because there is no need to allow space for walking between rows of plants, it is also possible to get better yields from beds by having less space between plants. Close growth of plant foliage in beds also helps to exclude weeds; and beds are much easier to cover, for example with netting against pests or with films or fleeces to encourage growth.

The optimum width for a bed is around 1.2m (4ft). If only I'd read up on this before setting out my allotment beds at 1.7m (5.6ft), which is just too far to plant, weed and water and harvest comfortably in the middle of the bed. At 1.2m, anything you need to do can be done from the path.

Beds can either simply be marked out or raised, enclosed with the edging material of your choice: wood, bricks, even inverted wine bottles. Raised beds are useful if you have sloping land, or no soil at all and want to start growing on, say, a concrete surface. In this case all the soil and soil improver needs to be brought in, but this gives you complete control over your growing medium.

The paths between beds (which should be around 0.5m/2ft wide) need to be low-maintenance and able to support plenty of foot traffic. Weeds will rapidly grow on any exposed ground and will invade even raised beds, so paths need to be protected from them. A mulch of chipped wood or straw on top of a base of newspaper looks attractive, but will need renewing from time to time because the weeds will always find a way through. Gravel is a more permanent but slightly less pretty option; and brick paving is sturdier still but needs more in the way of time and resources to build.

A final factor to consider with beds is orientation: ideally this should be north–south in order to minimize the shading effect of taller plants.

If you don't have room for beds, then anything edible can be grown in a container – whether it's a yoghurt pot with some basil in it, a posh terracotta planter from the garden centre or a stack of tyres being used for growing potatoes. There are two things to bear in mind when using containers: one is that the soil will need to be renewed every year. Containers don't have enough space to keep worms happy – they need a larger range – and therefore they won't be there to do their customary job of incorporating and transforming organic matter and improving soil structure. So the soil in a container will just become depleted over time if it is not renewed. The second issue with containers is watering. Plants in containers need three times more water than those planted out in deep soil, where moisture is retained better and their roots can reach down for water. But if containers are all you have room for, then chances are you'll be close at hand to watch and water regularly. Ideally, though, if you have room to build a few proper beds, they will provide more hassle-free growing than lots of containers.

Compost

Compost inspires great passion, and much discussion. I once couldn't resist buying a T-shirt with the slogan 'make compost not war', partly because it elevated such an ostensibly humble subject to geopolitical heights. I think people get excited about compost because there is a certain alchemy about it. Throw veg scraps and garden waste onto a heap and, in time, all is transformed by bugs and worms into sweet, dark crumbly stuff that does wonders for your soil and thus your plants. Compost also gets people going because it is such a blindingly obvious thing to do if you are growing organically and trying to do things sustainably: with a minimum of effort, it turns waste that would otherwise be burnt or landfilled into free soil improver, produced exactly where it needs to be applied.

Composting is rarely a complete solution to soil fertility, though: it is unlikely that most of us will be able to produce enough to keep all our soil in perfect shape. Unless you have a big acreage and some manure-producing livestock, you will most likely have to 'import' soil fertility by buying in compost or manure from outside (see also p. 42, 'Preparing and managing the ground'). However, there are so many plus points to composting that everyone who is growing anything should have a heap.

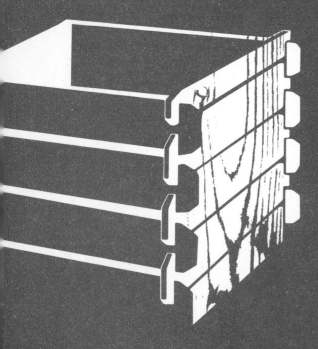

How composting works

In essence, composting is the liberation of nutrients from decaying matter. It is a managed process of natural recycling: a similar process, for example, happens completely naturally on a forest floor, where decaying leaves return fertility to the soil. A compost heap teems with life and activity: macro-organisms like worms, beetles and centipedes break the materials down and micro-organisms – bacteria and fungi – digest the composting materials, releasing the nutrients and completing the transformation to compost.

How to make compost

There are three main types of composting – the type you choose depends on what sort of 21st-Century Smallholder you are.

Cool composting

This is composting for most of us. It suits people with a garden or outside space who produce a bit of vegetable waste, grow some plants and read a few newspapers. The heap can be built up gradually and needs little attention. The downside is that it takes a while – usable compost is ready in about a year – and cool composting does not kill weed seeds. The key is to build a decent bin (see p. 50) and to get a good balance of 'greens' and 'browns' (see table on p. 51) to provide the right balance of elements that the decomposer organisms need. 'Greens' provide the nitrogen and 'browns' provide the carbon. Material should either be added in layers, or just mixed as you add it: so, for example, add some shredded newspaper with each handful of vegetable scraps. You can also add nitrogen-rich materials to 'activate' the heap: nettles, comfrey and human urine are particularly good. Peeing on newspaper gives the heap a carbon/nitrogen hit in one go, as well as perhaps providing some ideological satisfaction. Once the heap is full, and sufficient time has elapsed, you can either take off finished compost from the bottom of the heap or – with a multi-chambered heap – cover up the full heap to let it 'mature' and start a new one.

Hot composting

Hot composting is more labour-intensive and it also requires that you start with a cubic metre or so of fresh, mixed greens and browns, which is a lot. But it will provide finished compost much more quickly (in just a couple of months in summer) and the heat – generated by intense bacterial action – will kill weed seeds and disease organisms. So hot composting suits those who are doing a lot of growing or have generated a great deal of waste organic matter. The trick is to mix everything together – browns, greens, activators – cover the heap and then turn it after two weeks or so (or when it has cooled down). This makes sure that everything gets treated to the hot composting process and it also re-supplies the aerobic bacteria with air. The heap will need to be turned every two weeks or so; and care must be taken to make sure it's neither too dry nor too wet. Commercially available compost 'tumblers' can make it easier to turn and manage a hot heap.

Worm composting

If you have only a minimal outside space or none at all, worm composting might be the answer. Worms can eat half their own body weight in vegetable waste every day and turn it into worm casts (which are, in effect, excellent compost) and a liquid that can be turned into plant food. So if all you have to compost is veg scraps and the odd bit of window-box plant, a wormery could be the answer. To get started you can either buy complete kits (which include worms) or go the DIY route by modifying a small plastic bin and scoring some worms from a muck heap or fishing tackle shop. The worms you want are called 'brandling' or 'tiger' worms and they are smaller than earthworms with a distinctive striped appearance. For a home-made wormery, use a plastic bin with a lid and start with a layer of gravel topped with a board drilled with drainage holes. The bin should also have a few drainage holes drilled in the bottom. Then add some 'bedding' for the worms, such as shredded card or paper. Throw in the worms, then add veg scraps (little and often to start with) and keep the heap covered with damp card or paper to stop it drying out. You can empty the heap maybe once or twice a year, taking off the uncomposted layer and the worms (which then go back in the bin) to get at the good stuff. Commercial worm bins have multiple chambers that make it easier to get at the compost and the valuable liquid the worms create.

Finally, leafmould should get a mention. Anyone who lives under trees will have the annual problem of gathering and disposing of the leaves. There are usually too many to add to a standard cool compost heap, but fortunately there's a perfect way of dealing with them. Piling the leaves up in a square enclosure made of wire netting attached to strong poles, and compressing the leaves when they are added, eventually creates leafmould. The process takes around two years but the resulting material is an excellent soil conditioner.

Getting a compost bin

There is a bewildering array of heap-building options for the novice composter. The best rule of thumb is to aim for a main composting space of around 1m x 1m x 1m and, if possible, have a multi-chambered heap. So the optimum heap with three chambers might take up, say, a 4m x 1m (13ft x 3.25ft) space in your garden. This is a lot for a small garden, so for many of us a single heap will do the trick. You can buy all manner of posh compost bins (there's even one that looks like a beehive, for goodness' sake) but this is one area where DIY really is within reach of all of us. As I discovered, three scavenged pallets held together with cable ties will make an excellent heap, as will a low structure made of straw bales (which can themselves be composted afterwards). A compost heap also needs a lid (old carpet held down with bricks is fine) and a bit of drainage: if it's standing on an impermeable surface it should be built on a mesh base laid on top of bricks or stones. You can make compost in wheelie bins or stacks of tyres; however, tall heaps made of impermeable materials like this need aeration at the bottom to stop everything going anaerobic and smelly.

Composting materials

ACTIVATORS	GREENS	BROWNS	DON'T COMPOST
Urine	Fruit and veg scraps	Cardboard	Perennial weeds (e.g.
Nettles	Grass clippings	Newspaper	dock, bindweed,
Comfrey leaves	Young weeds	Straw	couch grass, ground
Poultry manure	Old plants	Egg boxes	elder)
	Teabags	Paper bags	Thorny or woody
	Coffee grounds	Chopped brassica	material*
	Hair	stems	Fat, oil or meat
	Vacuum cleaner	Autumn leaves	Cat and dog faeces
	contents	Sawdust	Diseased vegetables
	Herbivore manures	Bracken	Glossy magazines

* Although such material will eventually produce excellent compost in very tall bins if left for several years.

Sowing, planting and propagation

So now you have beds full of beautiful soil: time to throw in some seeds and see what happens! You can do that, and stuff will happen – but a few pointers will help you to be more successful.

Most things can be sown in situ (where they are going to grow to full size), but many species benefit from spending their formative weeks either in a dedicated seedbed or in a protected environment where tender seedlings can be kept safe from the ravages of weather and pests.

What this means for the 21st-Century Smallholder is that a bit of planning is necessary, because you need somewhere to put seedlings before they go into their final 'planted out' position. In an ideal world, we would all have a greenhouse which, once it has finished housing your seedlings in the spring, can also be home to summer and winter crops for which our climate is just too harsh. However, we don't all have the money or the space. I found out that a small 'lean-to' greenhouse just a few feet high will house enough seed trays for an allotment-scale veg-gardening operation; failing that, an improvised 'cold frame' (maybe an old window frame on a wooden box) or even a few windowsills inside your house will do the trick.

There are no hard-and-fast rules about what should be sown directly and what should be raised before planting out. Some gardeners prefer to raise everything up to a good size before planting out; others are more flexible. Some general guidelines:

Sow in situ: root vegetables, such as carrots, parsnips, radishes and turnips, because they don't transplant easily; or 'cut-and-come-again' crops like lettuce, whose leaves can be cut when the plants are young.

Sow in seedbeds or trays: leeks and brassicas, because the seedlings mature slowly and take up valuable space in your vegetable beds.

Sow under cover: frost-tender, 'half-hardy' plants such as tomatoes and cucumbers.

In situ

Sowing techniques vary enormously according to the type of plant. A 'tilth' of fine, light soil is important.

Small seeds (e.g. lettuce, brassicas) generally need only around 2cm/0.5in of soil covering them once sown. These should be sown 'thinly' (not too many seeds together), then 'thinned' as they grow to create the final spacing. Thinning is an unsettling business: it feels strange to uproot and discard your carefully nurtured seedlings. However, the good news is that most thinnings make excellent eating and can provide intensely tasty, early salads.

Bigger seeds (e.g. beans, peas, courgettes, sweetcorn) can be planted out at their final spacing, usually at a greater depth than small seeds.

It is worth noting at this point that the spacings on seed packets are often designed for traditional row cultivation and sometimes for 'competition' size, rather than optimum eating size, which is often smaller. Joy Larkcom, the author of *Grow Your Own Vegetables,* the bible of vegetable-growing, recommends equidistant spacing (which is also ideal for bed systems). Many seed packets suggest a spacing between seeds and a further, often larger, spacing between rows. Larkcom suggests adding these two figures together and halving them to create the ideal space between plants. So if a packet suggests that the final position is 20cm/8in apart in rows 30cm/12in apart, the equidistant spacing between plants will be 25cm/10in.

Seedbeds and trays

Seedbeds can be difficult for the small-space gardener because they hog valuable growing space; and because they are outside, the seedlings in them are vulnerable to the weather and pests. Seed trays (which can be used indoors or in a greenhouse) are more flexible; and module trays (seed-tray inserts with individual cells) are even better, because they allow seedlings to be transplanted without disturbing their roots and with a ready-made 'plug' of soil to put in the ground. Egg boxes make good, cheap module trays. The individual compartments can be torn out and planted when the seedling is ready; its roots will grow through the cardboard as it rots away. Module trays will need regular, attentive watering because they dry out quickly. Some plants (e.g. tomatoes) will benefit from 'potting on' into larger pots, giving them a chance to develop further before being planted out.

Under cover

Some plants will need to be started under cover, either indoors/heated or just protected. Guidelines can be found in 'Meet the fruit and veg' on pp. 64–95. If they are indoors, good access to natural light is essential: seedlings with insufficient light will strain towards it and become 'leggy' (too long) and weak. As they grow – and as the season progresses – seedlings can be 'hardened off', which means gradually exposing them to the elements so they don't get a fatal shock when planted out in the open. In practice, this either means putting seed trays outside in the daytime as the weather warms up; or opening the doors or vents of a greenhouse or cold frame.

Growing media

If you're not using a seedbed, then you'll need something to fill the seed and module trays. An issue for the environmentally conscious gardener is that many commercial 'potting' composts contain peat (a non-renewable resource) and artificial fertilizer. So it's worth looking around for eco-friendly composts, which tend to be made from coir or from peat filtered from natural moorland rainwater runoff. Your own garden compost, mixed with a bit of sand and soil, will ultimately make an excellent growing medium for seedlings.

Successional sowing

It's worth thinking about this from the outset (I didn't). If you sow all your seeds at once you'll get a glut of produce; and if you save some seeds, they might not last until the next season and may therefore go to waste. Sowing little and often, however, means that you get a longer, more reliable supply of produce. This technique is particularly important for fast-growing vegetables that are best eaten young: lettuces, radishes, salad rocket, dwarf French beans, spinach. The trick is to wait until the first sowing has germinated before putting in the next.

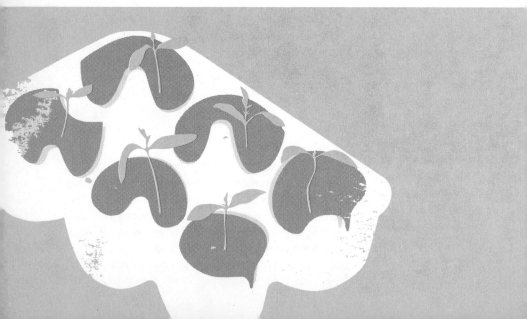

Organic gardening practices

Everything discussed about growing in this chapter could be described as an 'organic' practice. However, there are some specific practices that are essential to successful edible gardening without artificial fertilizers, pesticides and herbicides.

Rotation

At the heart of organic farming as well as just edible gardening is crop rotation. Different crops make different demands on the soil, and if they are planted in the same place year after year, the soil becomes exhausted and 'sick'. So the classic crop rotation order of legumes→brassicas→roots→onions takes advantage of each group's feeding habits.

The other key reason for rotating is to avoid the build-up of diseases that attack specific crops. Clubroot, for example, which attacks brassicas, can stay in the ground for twenty years. To avoid these diseases, as a general rule there should be a three-year gap before returning one of the main rotation groups to the same bed. These are summed up in the table below, together with the other main vegetable groups.

FAMILY	VEGETABLES	FEEDING HABITS
Main rotation groups (most important to rotate)		
Legumes	Beans, clover, peas	'Fixes' atmospheric nitrogen in root nodules, providing nutrition for following crops.
Brassicas	Broccoli, Brussels sprouts, cabbage, cauliflower, kale, rocket, swede, turnip	Hungry feeders.
Umbellifers	Carrots, celeriac, celery, parsley, parsnips	Take nutrients from deeper in the soil.
Alliums	Garlic, leeks, onions	Hardy, need little feeding.
Nightshades (*Solanaceae*)	Aubergines, peppers, potatoes, tomatoes	Hungry feeders.
OTHER GROUPS		
Cucurbits	Courgettes, cucumbers, pumpkins, squash	Hungry feeders.
Beet family (*Chenopodiaceae*)	Beetroot, chard, spinach	Need fertile soil, can be rotated with carrots and parsnips.
Lettuce family (*Asteraceae*)	Cardoon, chicory, globe and Jerusalem artichokes, lettuce, salsify and scorzonera	Like well-drained soils. Perennial cardoon and globe artichoke can be planted in own space; Jerusalem artichoke, salsify and scorzonera can be grouped with roots; lettuce can go anywhere.

So it is ideal to have at least four vegetable beds to allow for the main rotation groups to be moved around from year to year: having five would give potatoes their own dedicated space, and six would give even more flexibility. However, crops with similar habits can be grouped together – for example, potatoes and cucurbits, both of which are heavy feeders.

Green manures

This is the practice of growing a crop whose sole purpose is to help the soil. Green manures can be added into a crop rotation, conditioning the ground between plantings. They add fertility with either their foliage or nitrogen fixed at their roots; and they also provide cover and structure that prevents nutrients being leached out of the soil by rain. When required, they are either dug into the soil or hoed off and left on the surface for the worms to deal with: this should be done up to four weeks before planting the next crop. Green manures won't provide all the fertility the following crop needs: but having something growing in your vacant veg bed is much better than having bare soil. Many of the crops will stay in the ground through the winter, protecting and conditioning the soil. Others work as 'catch crops' to fill the gaps between a crop being cleared and another sown.

Some of the main green manures and their uses are summarized in the table below:

PLANT	USES
Clover	Fixes nitrogen. Sow from early spring to late summer – prefers light soil.
Field beans	Fixes nitrogen. Sow in autumn to overwinter – prefers heavy soil.
Winter tares	Fixes nitrogen. Sow in late summer/autumn to overwinter – avoid dry soils.
Grazing rye	Improves soil structure and boosts organic matter. Sow in late summer and autumn to overwinter – suits most soils.
Mustard	Adds nitrogen when foliage is dug in. Sow in early spring/late summer. Suits most soils.

Mulching

Mulching simply describes the practice of covering the ground with a layer of material: it can be anything from gravel to cardboard, comfrey to compost. The main purpose of mulching is to control weeds by excluding light; it also helps conserve moisture in the soil and can also release nutrients into it; and mulches can keep crops clean and are also an important feature of 'no-dig' gardening (see p. 45). Some mulches and their uses:

MATERIAL	USE
Compost	Apply around established vegetable crops in the growing season to provide nutrients and suppress weeds.
Well-rotted manure	Use around hungry feeding plants when they are putting on growth.
Straw	Around fruit (e.g. strawberries) to keep the fruit clean; or under squash and pumpkins.
Hay	Controls weeds and keeps in moisture around fruit trees and bushes.
Plastic film	Controls weeds, keeps in moisture: crops can be planted through the film for maximum weed control.
Wilted comfrey leaves	Release nutrients.
Cardboard, old carpet, thick newspaper, chipped wood	Control weeds and keep in moisture.

More advanced techniques

Pests thrive in vegetable gardens because they have a large supply of their favourite food in the same place. A big brassica patch, for example, is heaven for the cabbage white butterfly. However, simply putting in plants known to attract pest predators will not necessarily solve the problem; and trying to attract precisely the right kind of predator at precisely the right time is a complex business. It's easier to seek to get a healthy biodiversity going in the garden (see Chapter 4) and to make sure you grow a good range of food crops. 'Intercropping' has more proven pest-control value: alternating carrots with four rows of onions will deter carrot root fly whilst the onion leaves are growing. And intercropping can also be used to get more productivity out of the edible garden – for example, by planting fast-growing spring onions amongst slow-maturing leaves. Undercropping works with tall plants that don't exclude too much light: a classic combination is to train trailing pumpkins around blocks of sweetcorn plants.

Weed, pest and disease control

After the different approach to soil fertility (natural fertilizer and soil improvement vs. artificial fertilizer), the next most obvious difference between organic and 'conventional' gardening (and agriculture) is the attitude to weed and pest control. The 'conventional' approach uses herbicides and pesticides to control weeds and insect pests. This gets instant results, which is great, but brings with it a range of problems. Pesticides will kill pest predators as well as the pests themselves, bringing the possibility of even bigger pest populations in the coming year and therefore creating an escalating cycle of pesticide use. Then there is the question of potential residues in food: there seems to me to be little point in growing your own produce for its gourmet and nutritional value if it is going to be doused in poisons through the growing season.

Weed control

Unlike fragile, over-bred annual vegetables, weeds need no pampering and tender loving care: they are perfectly adapted to their soil and climate. As such, they have a major head start on your crops. It is, of course, seriously tempting to zap them with some high-tech concoction when you see them colonizing your edible garden during the frenzied growing season of late spring. However, the most sustainable way to deal with them is by doing strategic things to deny them habitat or by physical control (see table on pp. 59–60).

A crucial piece of weed intelligence is the difference between annual and biennial weeds, and perennial weeds. The former grow, flower and set seed either within a year or two years. Because their roots are shallower than perennials, they are easier to control by hoeing and therefore your focus should be on catching them before they set seed. (Nothing is more disheartening than dislodging a big weed plant only to watch hundreds of seeds spill all over your vegetable beds.) Perennial weeds persist for longer and have impressive survival strategies that make them very difficult to eradicate. Hedge bindweed, for example, can regenerate from the tiniest fragment of root buried in the soil. To eradicate perennial weeds completely needs either long-term mulching, persistent effort to remove every bit of root or rhizome, or just resigned acceptance and plenty of hoeing and hand-weeding.

Common weeds

NAME	TYPE	COMMENTS
Chickweed, fat hen, groundsel, hairy bittercress	Annual	Relatively easy to control. Hoeing, mulching, close spacing of crops will do the job. Weeds can be composted as long as they have not gone to seed.
Burdock, hogweed	Biennial	Strategies as above.
Couch grass, ground elder, bindweed	Perennial	Harder to control. Dig out and remove all roots; mulch over a full growing season or more; or simply hoe and weed regularly. Avoid composting these perennial weeds: burn them instead.
Dandelion, bramble, nettle	Perennial	Also hard to control. However, these three are edible and useful: nettles are a good compost activator and plant food source and dandelions attract insects as well as making good salads.

Weed strategies

PREVENTION

Don't dig	Digging brings weed seeds to the surface, where they germinate. A 'no-dig' system (see p. 45) avoids this problem.
Rotate	Some crops (potatoes, squashes) suppress weeds well; others (alliums) are susceptible to them. Crop rotation prevents a uniform build-up of weeds in your vegetable-growing area.
Use a 'stale seedbed'	This involves preparing a seedbed two or three weeks before sowing: exposed weed seeds germinate and can be easily hoed off before the crop goes in.
Space plants closely	Closer spacing of leafy crops excludes the light that many weeds need.
Start plants off in modules	Planting vegetables out when they are better established gives them a stronger chance of competing with weeds.
Mulching	From the extreme strategy of growing everything through black plastic film to applying a covering of organic matter, mulching is an effective way to control weeds.

CURE

Mulching	If you are able to 'set aside' a patch of ground, a light-excluding mulch will clear all annual weeds in around six months in the growing season and even perennials after 2–3 years.
Hand weeding	The most painstaking but effective way to get weeds out from amongst your crops; made easier by a narrow-bed system (see p. 46). Using a hand tool is essential to remove deep-rooting perennials like dandelion.
Hoeing	Quick and easy way to chop down annual weeds, which can then be left to wither on the soil surface or can be composted. Will also weaken (but not remove) perennials.
Flame weeding	Highly targeted but rather high-tech way of dealing with annuals and perennials.
Permanent war	A regular combination of mulching, hand weeding and hoeing is the only non-chemical way to deal with established weeds during the growing season: however, good prevention strategies and mulching will keep the effort needed to a minimum.

Pests and diseases

There is a bewildering and potentially depressing array of bugs and illnesses that can scupper your edible-gardening plans. However, they will only be truly devastating if you're just growing one thing: a garden monoculture of nothing but potatoes, for example. Organic and permaculture growing techniques focus strongly on prevention, by creating the healthiest possible environment for both flora and fauna. They try, as much as possible, to create a diverse, balanced ecosystem in which pests are dealt with by natural predators and diseases prevented by good husbandry. Chapter 4 outlines the broad techniques for creating such a balanced ecosystem and it also lists some of the predatory creatures that should be encouraged.

It is not necessary to know every single pest and disease in detail; however, it's worth being familiar with the most common ones. The table below lists common pests and diseases, while the table on p. 63 outlines the main techniques for preventing and curing pest and disease problems. In 'Meet the fruit and veg' (pp. 64–95), plant-specific pests and diseases – and strategies to deal with them – are outlined.

COMMON EDIBLE-GARDENING PESTS	
What they are	**What they do**
Caterpillar and insect larvae	Eat leaves, particularly of brassica plants (cabbage white); also eat roots and tubers (carrot root fly).
Slugs and snails	Eat leaves, young plants, fruit.
Aphids	Suck the sap from plants.
Beetles and weevils	Eat young plants, flowerheads, buds.
Birds	Eat seedlings, fruit and fruit buds, green veg.
Mammals	Rabbits eat veg; foxes, dogs, cats disturb ground; moles cause structural mayhem (but denote a healthy earthworm population).
COMMON DISEASES	
Potato blight	Destroys foliage and rots tubers.
Clubroot	Deforms roots and causes poor growth in brassicas.
Cucumber mosaic virus	Kills cucurbits.

Slugs

A special mention must go to slugs, every organic gardener's arch-foe. They deligh
in the organic matter-rich environment that we create, eat almost anything we grow
and there is no non-chemical strategy that will stop them completely. The mos
damaging slugs are the small ones that live just below the soil surface; most slugs also
feed at night, making control even more difficult. Here are some slug strategies:

Hunting	Go out at night with a headtorch and tongs, then put them in a bucket and fill it with boiling water. Compost the dead slugs. Doing this on several consecutive nights will severely deplete a garden's slug population but it is hard work.
Trapping	Bowls full of beer sunk into your veg beds will soon fill with happily expiring slugs, who have a taste for the stuff (their only endearing characteristic). The bowls (or commercial slug traps) need to be refreshed regularly, otherwise they will become too horrific to approach. Another trapping technique is to leave a long, heavy piece of wood or slate somewhere on the veg bed: slugs will congregate underneath this in the daytime and can be removed and dispatched.
Biowarfare	Commercially available parasitic nematode worms can be applied to slug-infested areas. This can be expensive for big areas but is good for raised beds (but not for heavy clay soils). The encouragement of frogs and ducks, both slug gourmets, can help control populations, although frogs will not thrive where there are cats.
Barriers	Rough material around susceptible plants can impede slugs' progress. Eggshells, special slime-sucking grits and ground ash from fires are all used. Cloches made from sawn-off plastic bottles can protect young plants.
Disruption	Slugs and snails pick up trails they have used before: hoeing around plants disrupts these and makes life harder for the slugs.

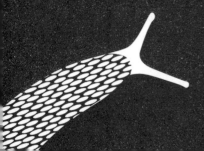

Pest and disease strategies

PREVENTION	
Encourage nature	Planting and creating habitats that encourage beneficial creatures (see Chapter 4) will go a long way towards creating an environment in which pest control happens naturally.
Rotate	Crop rotation (see p. 55) prevents the build-up of soil-borne diseases.
Build good soil	Building good, healthy soil will create healthy plants that are more resistant to disease.
Put things in the right place	Putting plants where they will get the balance of nutrients, sunlight, shelter and water they need will also help them to fight disease.
Be there	'The best fertilizer is the farmer's footprint': this traditional saying can be adapted to pest and disease prevention. Regular attention helps in catching problems early on.
Timing	Planting some crops at particular times can help them to avoid pest and disease problems (for specific crops see 'Meet the fruit and veg', pp. 64–95.)
Interplanting	A mix of vegetables and flowers can deter or confuse some pests.
Hygiene	Keeping gardening kit clean reduces the risk of disease transmission.
Cultivar choice	Buy disease-resistant cultivars; be wary of plants from unknown sources.
Deterrents	Bird-scarers work if changed from time to time. Human hair and male urine will deter foxes.
Barriers	Cloches – protect from slugs and birds. Netting – keeps birds off fruit (although make sure gaps are big enough for pollinating insects); also keeps cabbage white butterflies off brassicas. Fences – low barriers keep out carrot root fly; bigger fences necessary for mammals.
CURE	
Physical removal	Removing pests individually (see slugs, p. 62) can be effective; and clearing diseased or infested plants can prevent problems spreading.
Biological control	Insects and invertebrates – a range of predators can be deliberately introduced to deal with specific pest species. Bigger creatures – chickens will clear pests from the ground; frogs, ducks and slow-worms will eat slugs.
Chemical control	There is a small range of 'natural' pesticides permitted under organic rules. See the Soil Association website to find a listing of these.

Meet the fruit and veg

This section gives basic cultivation information for more than sixty fruits and vegetables. At the beginning of each entry are ratings which score the produce against a number of criteria relevant to the 21st-Century Smallholder looking to grow things at home or in a small space. These ratings are also summarized in the at-a-glance table on pp. 24–7.

Vegetables

ARTICHOKE, GLOBE

This plant has advantages and disadvantages for the 21st-Century Smallholder. It's perennial (and therefore low-maintenance), beautiful to look at and it's a gourmet vegetable, expensive to buy. But it takes up a vast amount of space, with a single plant growing up to 1.5m (5ft) tall and spreading up nearly a metre (40in). So this is a crop for those blessed with a lot of space, or those who value aesthetics over yield.

Soil, position, climate: doesn't like heavy, wet soils. Needs a sunny site, ideally sheltered.

Cultivation: planting from seed is difficult: it is best to grow from offsets (sections of shoot and root from an established plant). Plants crop for around three years so it is best to keep taking offsets to guarantee continuity. Mulch to control weeds.

Sow/plant: plant offsets in April.

Spacing: 1.25m (4ft) each way.

Harvest: July–September.

Pests and diseases: few problems.

Key: Space Time Gourmet Season Hassle Beauty

ARTICHOKE, JERUSALEM

Very different from the globe artichoke (you eat the tuber rather than the flower head); but Jerusalem artichokes offer similar advantages and disadvantages in that they take up a lot of space but are excellent eating. The plants additionally make a good windbreak, suppress weeds and, like potatoes, condition the soil well because of their fibrous roots. You will, however, need a lot of room to get a worthwhile yield out of this crop.

Soil, position, climate: tolerates most soils and will manage in partial shade.
Cultivation: plant tubers. Earth up stems in summer for more support, remove flower buds and water in summer to increase yield. Cut stems down to 15cm (6in) when leaves wither in the autumn.
Sow/plant: February–March; plant tubers 15cm (6in) deep.
Spacing: 45cm (18in) each way.
Harvest: October–February; tubers don't store well so should be eaten straight away. Save good ones for replanting.
Pests and diseases: few problems.

ASPARAGUS

This is the ultimate gourmet vegetable, providing a superb eating experience in a short early-summer season. It's perennial, needing little attention once established, and will crop for up to twenty years, but it will take at least two years from planting before you get your first harvest. Asparagus also needs a dedicated bed, making it suited to larger gardens (although it can be grown in large containers or raised beds).

Soil, position, climate: needs free-draining, slightly alkaline soil; doesn't like cold and wet climates. The soil must be clear of perennial weeds.
Cultivation: it can be raised from seed but buying one-year-old crowns reduces the time to harvest from three to two years.
Sow/plant: March–April (crowns). Work organic matter into the soil before planting crowns 20cm (8in) deep, 45cm (18in) apart, in a mound of soil in the bottom of the hole or trench.
Spacing: 30cm (12in) each way.
Harvest: April–June. Cut spears 5cm (2in) below soil level when 15cm (6in) tall.
Pests and diseases: asparagus beetle, slugs.

AUBERGINE

Strictly speaking, aubergines have no place in a book largely concerned with outdoor produce for temperate climates. Tropical plants, they grow best indoors or under glass, unless you live somewhere exceptionally warm and sunny. However, this makes them ideal for people with little space, because the compact plants can provide an interesting crop from a windowsill.

- **Soil, position, climate**: need rich compost if in containers and reasonably fertile soil. Very warm, sheltered site needed for growth outdoors: temperatures of 25–30°C give the best yield and aubergines also like humidity.
- **Cultivation**: sow indoors or in a heated greenhouse in spring at 20°C. Pot on into small pots then move into growbags, beds under cover or 20cm (8in) pots when first flowers appear. Allow only 4–6 fruits to grow on each plant.
- **Sow/plant**: March–April (indoors or heated greenhouse).
- **Spacing**: 40cm (16in) each way if in beds.
- **Harvest**: August–September.
- **Pests and diseases**: whitefly, aphids.

BEANS, BROAD

Broad beans are a perfect crop for the home-based, novice grower. They do need a bit of space, but they are hardy, easy to grow, fix nitrogen in the soil and provide a copious, delicious crop that changes through its season. The pods can be eaten when very young; thereafter the beans are great raw or briefly boiled; and end-of-season, tougher beans can be dried or used in soups and stews. It is very hard to match the freshness of your own crop, even at the best farmers' markets.

- **Soil, position, climate**: likes well-dug, fertile soil; thrives in cool climate.
- **Cultivation**: plant direct, 4–5cm (1.5–2in) deep in either autumn or spring. Autumn or early spring sowings can avoid blackfly attack. Pinch out the tops when plants are in full flower to reduce the attraction to blackfly.
- **Sow/plant**: October–December (outside, autumn-sown); February–April (outside, spring-sown). Plant seeds 5cm (2in) deep.
- **Spacing**: 23cm (9in) each way.
- **Harvest**: May–September.
- **Pests and diseases**: blackfly (black bean aphid), pea and bean weevil, chocolate spot, mice.

Key: Space Time Gourmet Season Hassle Beauty

BEANS, FRENCH

This is a crop that can provide very good yields from small spaces. Dwarf and climbing varieties are available; and climbing varieties in particular, with their attractive flowers, can be trained well over 2m (6ft) high to add colour to the garden in summer. French beans are not as hardy as broad or runner beans, so need to be planted later or started off under cover.

- **Soil, position, climate**: reasonably fertile soil and a warm, sunny, sheltered spot.
- **Cultivation**: sow under cover in spring or outdoors in early summer. Never sow in cold weather or wet soil. Climbing cultivars need to be trained up tall canes or wigwams.
- **Sow/plant**: April–June (outside). Plant seeds 5cm (2in) deep.
- **Spacing**: 23cm (9in) each way.
- **Harvest**: June–October. Keep picking to ensure a heavy crop.
- **Pests and diseases**: blackfly (black bean aphid), bean seed fly, slugs.

BEANS, RUNNER

A staple of edible gardening in Britain, runner beans are hardier than French beans and provide the same floral beauty in the summer as well as a tasty and copious crop. They will climb over 3m (10ft) and provide a useful screen at the height of their growing season. The pods are eaten before the seeds develop. As with all legumes, freshness is crucial so your own crop is likely to provide the best possible eating experience.

- **Soil, position, climate**: need fertile, moisture-retentive soil (that also allows the plants to root deeply) in a sheltered, sunny spot.
- **Cultivation**: sow direct late spring to early summer. Train up double rows of canes, cane wigwams, trellises.
- **Sow/plant**: May–July (outside). Plant seeds 5cm (2in) deep.
- **Spacing**: 15cm (6in) each way or in rows 30cm (12in) apart.
- **Harvest**: July–October. Keep picking to ensure a heavy crop.
- **Pests and diseases**: blackfly (black bean aphid), bean seed fly, slugs.

Key: 4 (excellent)  3 2 █ 1 (not so good)

BEETROOT

With a good cropping season and the ability to store well, beetroot is a handy feature of the edible garden. Also on the plus side are its good looks, the fact that it can be eaten at any stage of growth and that the first tasty, nutritious beetroot of the year really is a harbinger of summer. Beetroot is relatively easy to grow and puts up with cooler climates. A large range of cultivars is available.

* **Soil, position, climate**: likes an open sunny site and prefers lighter soil, although this is not essential.
* **Cultivation**: can be sown in modules under cover in late winter or outside from spring to summer. Needs watering in hot, dry weather.
* **Sow/plant**: February–March (under cover); March/April–June (outside).
* **Spacing**: 15cm (6in) each way. Spacing options vary for different cultivars.
* **Harvest**: June–October.
* **Pests and diseases**: few problems.

BROCCOLI, CALABRESE

Calabrese is what most of us call broccoli and it offers the edible gardener the chance of a valuable crop with a long summer season. Freshness is of paramount importance with calabrese, as its many nutrients decline rapidly after picking, so growing your own gives the best guarantee of goodness. However, like all brassicas, calabrese is victim to an army of potential pests and will need to be well protected (with fine netting) and cared for to ensure a successful crop.

* **Soil, position, climate**: will manage on less fertile soils than other brassicas and likes high nitrogen content (so a good crop to follow nitrogen-fixing legumes). Needs an open but sheltered site.
* **Cultivation**: sow in modules under cover (resents root disturbance so doesn't transfer well) or sow direct from April onwards. Water in hot weather.
* **Sow/plant**: March–April (under cover); April–July (outside).
* **Spacing**: 15cm (6in) each way. Spacing options vary for different cultivars.
* **Harvest**: June–October. Pick main head before flowers open; then pick side shoots.
* **Pests and diseases**: slugs and snails, cabbage white fly, mealy cabbage aphids, cabbage root fly, birds, caterpillars, flea beetle, clubroot.

BROCCOLI, SPROUTING

This is a vegetable of tremendous gourmet value that has the extra advantage of providing a fresh crop at a lean time in the growing year. The downside to sprouting broccoli is that it takes up a lot of space and its growing season is very long, so small-space gardeners will find it hogs too much of their valuable growing area. However, for those of us fortunate to have big gardens or allotments, this is a great crop for the food enthusiast.

* **Soil, position, climate**: likes rich soil, lots of nitrogen and protection from strong winds.
* **Cultivation**: sow in modules under cover (resents root disturbance so doesn't transfer well) or sow direct from April onwards.
* **Sow/plant**: March–April (under cover); April–May (outside).
* **Spacing**: 60cm (24in) each way.
* **Harvest**: January–April. Pick shoots regularly to ensure a good crop.
* **Pests and diseases**: slugs and snails, cabbage white fly, mealy cabbage aphids, cabbage root fly, birds, caterpillars, flea beetle, clubroot.

BRUSSELS SPROUTS

The Brussels sprout is a very hardy winter vegetable that provides a crop over a long season. Like many in the brassica family it has excellent nutritional and gourmet value; Brussels sprouts also offer an end-of-season treat from the sprout 'tops', eaten after the last sprouts have been picked. This crop is really only suitable for large gardens or allotments, because the plants are slow-growing and take up a great deal of space.

* **Soil, position, climate**: likes fertile soil with lots of nitrogen.
* **Cultivation**: sow in deep modules under cover or sow direct from March–April. Mulch with grass mowings if not growing well in mid-summer; remove yellowing leaves in winter. May need staking in the winter.
* **Sow/plant**: March (under cover); May (outside). Plant out late May–June.
* **Spacing**: 45–90cm (18in–3ft) apart each way, depending on cultivars.
* **Harvest**: September–March. Early-, mid- and late-season cultivars available.
* **Pests and diseases**: slugs and snails, cabbage white fly, mealy cabbage aphids, cabbage root fly, birds, caterpillars, flea beetle, clubroot.

CABBAGE

It hardly does justice to the cabbage to have just one entry. There's a cabbage for every season and each has its culinary delights. For the 21st-Century Smallholder, there are a few things worth bearing in mind: some cabbages, particularly the winter varieties, grow slowly and take up a lot of space. However, the more tender spring cabbages are smaller and can grow over winter. Certain varieties can be stored or pickled, if you're going for serious food independence.

- **Soil, position, climate**: likes an open site with rich fertile soil and lots of nitrogen. A cool-climate crop.
- **Cultivation**: varies according to variety; however, starting in module trays before planting out works well for most. Needs watering in dry weather. Cabbages will also need netting against their many flying predators.
- **Sow/plant**: August–September (spring varieties); February–March (under cover, summer varieties); May (autumn/winter varieties).
- **Spacing**: 30–50cm (12–20in) apart, depending on cultivars.
- **Harvest**: all year round, depending on variety.
- **Pests and diseases**: slugs and snails, cabbage white fly, mealy cabbage aphids, cabbage root fly, birds, caterpillars, flea beetle, clubroot.

CARDOON

Strictly for the committed edible gardener, cardoon cultivation takes a lot of space and quite a bit of time. It may be a perennial – closely related to the globe artichoke – but it's the stems of the cardoon rather than the flower heads that are eaten, so it is grown as an annual for eating. The plant is beautiful but very space-hungry: it grows to 1.5m (5ft) high and spreads to 90cm (3ft). And it needs lots of watering and then blanching to create an edible crop.

- **Soil, position, climate**: doesn't like heavy or wet soils and needs shelter and sunlight.
- **Cultivation**: can be raised and transplanted, or sown direct in spring. Needs regular watering. In the autumn, stems are blanched to make them tender for eating with a tight collar of cardboard or thick newspaper.
- **Sow/plant**: April.
- **Spacing**: 1.5m (5ft) each way.
- **Harvest**: October–December.
- **Pests and diseases**: few problems.

CARROTS

They can provide a fresh, home-grown crop nearly all year round and their long, narrow shape means big yields from small spaces. But carrots can be tricky to grow and don't like heavy soils, which can prevent the roots from growing properly. Early varieties mature more quickly and are eaten fresh in spring and summer; maincrops take longer and can be stored once lifted in the late summer and autumn.

- **Soil, position, climate**: light–medium, fertile soils, free of stones. Shelter needed for earlies.
- **Cultivation**: sow and thin to required spacing. Careful weeding needed in early stages, not too much water. Need barrier protection or careful timing of sowing to avoid carrot fly problems.
- **Sow/plant**: February–March (earlies); April–June (maincrop).
- **Spacing**: 7–15cm (3–6in) each way.
- **Harvest**: May–October. Store well too.
- **Pests and diseases**: carrot fly.

CAULIFLOWER

They may be terribly good for you but cauliflowers can be hard to grow and many varieties grow to sizes that are not suitable for the small-space gardener. They need steady growth through a long growing season in order for the 'curds' to develop properly, which means careful attention to watering, mulching and pest control. Summer and 'mini' varieties are best for small spaces.

- **Soil, position, climate**: reasonably fertile soil.
- **Cultivation**: start off in modules as they don't transplant well. Need watering and mulching in dry weather. Protect curds in autumn by tying up leaves.
- **Sow/plant**: October–February (earlies, under cover); March–May (summer–autumn varieties, under cover); May (winter varieties, outside).
- **Spacing**: 12.5cm (5in) each way for mini cauliflowers; 50–70cm (20–28in) for other varieties.
- **Harvest**: all year, depending on variety.
- **Pests and diseases**: slugs and snails, cabbage white fly, mealy cabbage aphids, cabbage root fly, birds, caterpillars, flea beetle, clubroot.

Key: ■ 4 (excellent) ■ 2 ■ 1 (not so good)

CELERIAC

Close to celery both botanically and in terms of flavour, celeriac can also be quite hard to grow well, because it needs a long period of uninterrupted growth. This means attentive watering and mulching during the growing season so the plant can develop a good-sized 'corm' (the plant's swollen stem-base).

- **Soil, position, climate**: likes an open site with rich, fertile soil. Will tolerate some shade.
- **Cultivation**: start in modules, pot on, then harden off before planting out in May. Needs watering in dry spells; lower leaves should be removed in mid-summer to expose the corm.
- **Sow/plant**: April–May (under cover); plant out in June.
- **Spacing**: 30cm (12in) each way.
- **Harvest**: September–May. Will survive through the winter.
- **Pests and diseases**: slugs, celery leaf miner, celery leaf spot.

CELERY

There are three options for the gourmet celery gardener. 'Trench' celery, the traditional English variety, offers better eating quality but is demanding of soil quality and needs labour-intensive earthing up or blanching. 'Self-blanching' celery – the type most commonly sold commercially – is less effort but not quite as tasty. 'Leaf' celery is hardy, vigorous and provides the celery flavour with less gardening effort than the other varieties.

- **Soil, position, climate**: needs rich, fertile soil that drains well and retains moisture.
- **Cultivation**: start out in modules under cover then plant out, retaining cover if there is a danger of frost. Slug-protection measures are essential, as is regular watering. Blanch trench celery with collars or by earthing up in the autumn.
- **Sow/plant**: April (under cover); plant out in June.
- **Spacing**: 30cm (12in) each way.
- **Harvest**: August–November.
- **Pests and diseases**: slugs, celery leaf miner, celery leaf spot.

CHARD

This is one of the 21st-Century Smallholder's ideal crops. It is easy to grow, good to eat, doesn't take up much space, looks great and crops for ages, even through the winter. Related to beetroot, and also known as Swiss chard or seakale beet, it has varieties in a range of striking colours for good ornamental value.

* **Soil, position, climate**: will manage on most soils, likes heavy ones best. Doesn't mind a bit of shade and tolerates drought.
* **Cultivation**: sow direct from late spring to early autumn, water and mulch if necessary.
* **Sow/plant**: April–August.
* **Spacing**: 30cm (12in) each way.
* **Harvest**: all year round. Cut leaves as needed.
* **Pests and diseases**: few problems.

CHICORY

Chicory is a complicated business. There is a range of varieties grown for eating in different ways: 'Witloof' and some red chicories (radicchio) are 'forced' in darkness for tender and tasty winter crops; 'Sugarloaf' chicories grow outside and make autumn crops of either whole plants or cut-and-come-again leaves.

* **Soil, position, climate**: reasonably fertile, deep soil.
* **Cultivation**: varies according to cultivar. Forcing process needs attention in the winter.
* **Sow/plant**: all year round, depending on variety.
* **Spacing**: 20–35cm (8–14in) each way.
* **Harvest**: all year round, depending on variety.
* **Pests and diseases**: few problems.

Key: ■ 4 (excellent) ■ 3 ■ 2 ■ 1 (not so good)

COURGETTES

We used to let them grow into huge, bland marrows: now we eat them smaller and call them courgettes. They are easy to grow and a good late-summer crop with many culinary uses. 'Bush' cultivars, suitable for containers and small spaces, make the vigorous, prolific plants viable for most gardens. The flowers are also edible.

- **Soil, position, climate**: reasonably fertile, well-drained soil.
- **Cultivation**: sow in pots under cover in late spring and transplant carefully when established; or sow direct in early summer. Very susceptible to frost. Water until established; mulch with hay or straw.
- **Sow/plant**: April–May (under cover) and plant out in June; June (outside).
- **Spacing**: 90cm (36in) (bush); 1.5m (4–6ft) (trailing).
- **Harvest**: July–October.
- **Pests and diseases**: slugs, cucumber mosaic virus.

CUCUMBER

Related to courgettes and pumpkins but less hardy, cucumbers are largely a greenhouse proposition unless you grow the spiny (and tastier) 'ridge' outdoor varieties. The business of indoor cucumber growing is complicated and tricky, so the directions below are for outdoor varieties.

- **Soil, position, climate**: reasonably fertile, well-drained soil.
- **Cultivation**: sow in pots or modules indoors or in a heated greenhouse in spring, or under cover in late spring. Harden off, then transplant when at three-leaf stage. Can be sown direct under cloches. Needs watering and mulching.
- **Sow/plant**: April–May (inside or heated greenhouse); May (under cover); June (direct, outside under cloches).
- **Spacing**: 75cm (30in) each way.
- **Harvest**: July–September.
- **Pests and diseases**: slugs, cucumber mosaic virus.

Key: ▊ Space ● Time ▌Gourmet ◆ Season ▌Hassle ✿ Beauty

ENDIVE

If you want the distinctive bitter note of flavour without the hassle of chicory cultivation, endive is an easier proposition. It is a cool-season plant that can provide a year-round crop; and it offers versatile eating because the seedlings, cut-and-come-again leaves, or whole plants can be eaten. There are curled (frisée) or broad-leaved varieties.

Soil, position, climate: reasonably fertile soil; summer varieties tolerate light shade, winter varieties need shelter and relatively infertile soil.
Cultivation: raise in modules under cover in spring and autumn or sow direct in summer. Can be grown under cover or cloched to provide a winter crop.
Sow/plant: April–May/August (under cover); June–July (outside).
Spacing: 30cm (12in).
Harvest: almost all year round, depending on variety.
Pests and diseases: slugs, aphids.

FENNEL

The type of fennel we find in the shops and eat for its aniseed-flavoured bulb is Florence fennel. It grows quickly but can bolt (go to seed) rather than form a bulb if sown too early. Florence fennel needs warm, moist conditions to thrive; however, it works well in small spaces and is a very attractive plant. The perennial herb fennel offers similar flavours for less effort (see p. 87).

Soil, position, climate: rich, well-drained, moisture-retentive soil.
Cultivation: sow bolt-resistant cultivars in spring under cover, or sow direct in mid-summer. Needs mulching, watering and earthing up when the bulbs are egg-sized.
Sow/plant: April–May (under cover); May–July (outside).
Spacing: 30cm (12in) each way.
Harvest: July–October.
Pests and diseases: slugs, bolting.

Key: 4 (excellent) 3 2 1 (not so good)

GARLIC

Although commercial garlic cultivation tends to happen only to the south of Britain, garlic is a hardy plant that needs a sustained period of cool weather to do well. It fits into the vegetable rotation along with onions and leeks and can provide copious yields from small spaces: in *The Edible Container Garden,* author Michael Guerra reports that a raised bed of one square metre can produce fifty-two bulbs.

Soil, position, climate: light, well-drained soil on an open site.
Cultivation: garlic is grown from cloves rather than seed: these are planted in the autumn or winter, flat end downwards, 2.5–10cm (1–4in) under the soil. Only minor watering and weeding needed.
Sow/plant: November–February.
Spacing: 18cm (7in) each way.
Harvest: July–August (bulbs can be dried and stored, depending on variety).
Pests and diseases: few problems.

KALE

Kale should be high on the first-time vegetable gardener's list of choices. It is easy to grow, highly nutritious, extremely hardy – providing a fresh crop right through the winter – and many varieties look delightful too. It also works better in small spaces than its brassica relative, cabbage, because the plants can stand in good condition for a long time, providing a constant 'cut-and-come-again' harvest from the leaves.

Soil, position, climate: rich, well-drained soil; however, kale is less demanding than other brassicas.
Cultivation: sow in modules in spring and plant out in mid-summer, water until established.
Sow/plant: April–May (outside or under cover); June (plant out).
Spacing: 30–70cm (12–28in) each way, depending on cultivar.
Harvest: August–April (cut leaves as needed. Flavour improved by frost).
Pests and diseases: all the usual brassica suspects – slugs and snails, cabbage white fly, mealy cabbage aphids, cabbage root fly, birds, caterpillars, flea beetle, clubroot – but kale is less susceptible to them.

Key: Space   Time   Gourmet   Season   Hassle   Beauty

KOHLRABI

A weirdly beautiful brassica that provides both gourmet and aesthetic interest and works well in small spaces. Kohlrabi also grows fast, is highly nutritious and less finicky and pest-prone than other brassicas. Its tennis-ball-sized swollen stem – like an exceptionally tasty turnip – is eaten, as are the leaves.

- **Soil, position, climate**: fertile, light soil (will tolerate heavy soil) and an open site.
- **Cultivation**: sow in modules or direct; successional sowing is recommended for a longer crop as the plants do not last long when ready to eat.
- **Sow/plant**: March–August (under cover or outside).
- **Spacing**: 25cm (10in) each way.
- **Harvest**: May–November (can also be stored).
- **Pests and diseases**: slugs and snails, cabbage root fly, birds, flea beetle, clubroot.

LEEKS

No edible garden should be without leeks. They provide superb flavour for the kitchen, stand through the winter and give a good yield from a relatively small area. Growing them takes a bit of effort but it's worth it for the reward of a reliable cold-season crop.

- **Soil, position, climate**: fertile, moisture-retentive, free-draining soil.
- **Cultivation**: sow in modules and plant out in mid-summer when 15–20cm (6–8in) tall, 'watering' each plant in to a 15–20cm (6–8in) deep hole. Water until established and weed as required.
- **Sow/plant**: March–May (outside); June (plant out).
- **Spacing**: 10–23cm (4–9in) each way. (As with onions, spacing influences size: smallest spacing will give a bigger yield of smaller leeks.)
- **Harvest**: September–May.
- **Pests and diseases**: few problems, however can be affected by slugs, leek moth, leek rust and cutworm.

LETTUCE

There's a lettuce for every garden and for every gardener. Lettuce is easy to grow and the huge range of varieties available means it can provide a fresh harvest almost all year round, as long as the plants can be protected in winter. 'Hearting' types such as Little Gem can be picked whole, whilst leaves of 'loose-leaf' varieties such as Catalogna can be picked as needed.

- **Soil, position, climate**: most soils OK as long as not too dry or poorly drained.
- **Cultivation**: sow under cover in spring for early crops or autumn for winter crops; sow successively outside for constant summer supply. Use thinnings as transplants if needed.
- **Sow/plant**: February–July (under cover); April–September (outside).
- **Spacing**: 15–35cm (6–14in) each way, depending on variety.
- **Harvest**: all year.
- **Pests and diseases**: lettuces are subject to a wide range of pests and diseases and problems, from slugs and snails to birds, aphids, fungal diseases, and bolting in summer heat.

ONIONS

This culinary staple is extremely easy to grow, albeit over a fairly long growing season. 'Maincrop' onions are not worth growing in the smallest spaces as it's hard to get a worthwhile crop and they tie up a vegetable bed for a long time. However, if you have a little more room they provide a good yield of high-quality produce for minimal effort; and if dried properly will keep for a long time in good condition.

- **Soil, position, climate**: reasonably fertile soil on an open site.
- **Cultivation**: can be grown from seed or 'sets' (small bulbs); latter is easier. Netting is needed in early stages if birds are a problem; onions must be weeded carefully.
- **Sow/plant**: February–March (seed, under cover); March–April (sets, outside). Or sow in August (plant sets in September–November) for overwintering early summer harvest.
- **Spacing**: 10–15cm (4–6in) each way. Spacing determines bulb size.
- **Harvest**: July–October (can be dried and stored thereafter).
- **Pests and diseases**: onion fly, onion white rot.

Key: ▌Space ◔ Time ▼ Gourmet ◆ Season ⌇ Hassle ✿ Beauty

ONIONS, SPRING

The onion option for the small-space gardener. Spring onions are selected varieties of bulb onion that are harvested early for their aromatic leaves and small bulbs. Like other salad crops, they are well-suited to containers and raised beds and can be grown closely together or amongst other crops.

* **Soil, position, climate**: reasonably fertile soil on an open site.
* **Cultivation**: successional sowings every 2–3 weeks in spring and summer give a long-lasting crop. Water and weed as needed.
* **Sow/plant**: March–June (outside, for summer/autumn crop); July–September (overwintering/early spring crop).
* **Spacing**: 1–2.5cm (0.5–1in) between seeds; sow in rows 10cm (4in) apart.
* **Harvest**: all year.
* **Pests and diseases**: onion fly, onion white rot.

PARSNIPS

Parsnips give a guarantee of fresh produce in the cold months and seem to have been designed for winter dishes. However, they are not appropriate for small spaces as the roots grow large and deep and their lengthy growing season ties up valuable space for a long time. Leaving a few parsnips to go to seed does, however, produce flowers that are hugely attractive to beneficial insects such as hoverflies.

* **Soil, position, climate**: well-cultivated soil, free of stones, in a sunny position.
* **Cultivation**: parsnip seeds are slow to germinate. One suggestion is to sow with radishes: when these are ready, the parsnips will be starting to show. Need careful weeding.
* **Sow/plant**: April–May.
* **Spacing**: 15–20cm (6–8in) each way.
* **Harvest**: September–April. (Parsnips are best after frost, and can either stay in the ground or be lifted and stored.)
* **Pests and diseases**: carrot fly, parsnip canker.

Key: ▨ 4 (excellent) ▨ 3 ▧ 2 ■ 1 (not so good)

PEAS

Once a staple food in Britain, peas are well suited to our climate and are one of the earlier crops in the growing year. Because the sugars in peas start turning to starch immediately after picking, it is impossible to match the quality of your own home-grown peas, no matter what the frozen-pea people say. Growing them takes a bit of effort, as most varieties need staking and support to provide a decent yield.

- **Soil, position, climate**: fertile soil with good drainage.
- **Cultivation**: sow direct. Peas need to be staked as they grow and provided with netting or mesh to climb up (although 'semi-leafless' types need little staking).
- **Sow/plant**: March–June (using early, second early and maincrop varieties).
- **Spacing**: 5cm (2in) apart, in broad drills.
- **Harvest**: June–October.
- **Pests and diseases**: birds, mice, pea and bean weevil.

PEPPERS AND CHILLIES

These tropical plants need heat and protection to thrive in our climate, which means being indoors, or in a greenhouse or polytunnel. However, they grow well in pots and small spaces and can provide a productive and ornamental crop for a sunny windowsill. Chillies grown here will still be hot; however, the hotter the variety, the longer the growing season.

- **Soil, position, climate**: reasonably fertile soil; ideally grown under cover.
- **Cultivation**: need 21°C to germinate. Grow in modules and then pot on into 10cm (4in) pots, then plant in final position when first flowers are showing.
- **Sow/plant**: March–April (indoors); plant out under cover around June.
- **Spacing**: 30–45cm (12–18in) apart.
- **Harvest**: August–October.
- **Pests and diseases**: aphids, red spider mite, whitefly.

Key: ▌Space ⬤ Time ❙ Gourmet ◆ Season ▼ Hassle ✿ Beauty

POTATOES

If you ever want to attempt self-sufficiency in food from a small space, then potatoes will be your staple carbohydrate in the British climate. They can be grown in deep containers giving big yields; however, grown thus they need much watering and feeding. For anyone with a reasonable amount of space, potatoes can provide either a fresh early crop or a main crop for storage later in the season. Potatoes are also good for conditioning the soil.

- **Soil, position, climate**: fertile, deep, slightly acid soil.
- **Cultivation**: seed potatoes are 'chitted' (sprouted) indoors (egg boxes are good for this) in late winter, then planted out in spring, 5cm (2in) below soil surface. Mulch or earth up as the plants grow to stop tubers being exposed to light (which makes them green and poisonous). Water when flowering.
- **Sow/plant**: February (chitting); March–May (planting out).
- **Spacing**: 30–35cm (12–16in) each way.
- **Harvest**: June–August (earlies); September (maincrop – can be stored).
- **Pests and diseases**: slugs, potato blight, potato cyst eelworm.

RADISHES (SALAD OR SUMMER)

Radishes can provide a fresh home-grown crop over a long season. Easy and quick to grow, they are a favourite with children (at least until they try to eat them and find the strong peppery flavour offputting!). Radishes are ideally suited to small containers and window boxes. They are best eaten when very fresh; another good reason for growing your own.

- **Soil, position, climate**: rich, light soil; need shade in summer to avoid bolting.
- **Cultivation**: sow in succession throughout the growing season. Don't over-water. Thin early (the thinnings are good to eat) and harvest as soon as mature.
- **Sow/plant**: February–September (outside, in succession, at two-week intervals); October–January (under cover, in succession as before).
- **Spacing**: 2.5–5cm (1–2in) apart.
- **Harvest**: all year.
- **Pests and diseases**: slugs, brassica pests.

RHUBARB

It may be eaten as a fruit, but it's classed as a vegetable. Rhubarb is a low-maintenance, high-yield perennial crop, perfect for the lazy or novice gardener. The plants take up a great deal of space, but one is usually enough to keep a family in rhubarb through its season. Responding to increasing day length rather than heat, it is the first 'fruit' of the British growing season.

- **Soil, position, climate**: will manage on most soils but doesn't like shade.
- **Cultivation**: easiest to grow from 'sets' or crowns. Plant these in autumn or late winter and water until established. Plants can be divided once established, allowing for some to be 'forced' with a pot or bucket in February to create more tender shoots. Forced crowns should be left for two years.
- **Sow/plant**: October–November/ February–March (plant crowns).
- **Spacing**: 90cm (3ft) each way.
- **Harvest**: January–March (forced), January–July. (Don't harvest until second year after planting.)
- **Pests and diseases**: few problems.

ROCKET

This is a 'no-brainer' for the first-time edible gardener. Rocket is easy and fast to grow, perfect for small spaces and containers and extremely tasty, pepping up the dullest of salads. Salad rocket is faster-growing, whilst the perennial wild rocket grows more slowly but has a more pungent flavour. If rocket is left to flower, the small blooms attract bees and are also edible.

- **Soil, position, climate**: will manage on most soils.
- **Cultivation**: can be sown almost all year round, under cover in the coldest months. Ready to cut leaves in 3–4 weeks. Rocket bolts quickly in hot weather – and the leaves become bitter – so avoid sowing (or cut quickly).
- **Sow/plant**: February–June/late August–September (outside); December–January (under cover).
- **Spacing**: 15cm (6in) each way.
- **Harvest**: all year round.
- **Pests and diseases**: few problems; include in the brassica rotation.

Key: Space Time Gourmet Season Hassle Beauty

SORREL

As a perennial, sorrel is perfect for the low/no-effort edible gardener. Its value – apart from easy maintenance – is that it provides one of the first fresh crops of the growing season. Its sharp flavour goes well with eggs and creamy sauces. Leaves cut earlier in the year taste best.

- **Soil, position, climate**: will manage on most soils.
- **Cultivation**: sow direct in autumn and spring; remove flower spikes to get more leaves (or let it self-seed). Renew plants after 3–4 years.
- **Sow/plant**: October–November/ March–April.
- **Spacing**: 30cm (12in) each way.
- **Harvest**: March–November (cut leaves).
- **Pests and diseases**: slugs, aphids.

SPINACH

Popeye was right – it's good stuff. And perfectly suited to window boxes and containers as well as bigger gardens. Spinach grows fast and is a versatile and nutritious leafy vegetable, best by far when fresh out of the ground. It prefers cool temperatures and has a tendency to run to seed in hot weather.

- **Soil, position, climate**: fertile, moisture-retentive soil on an open site (but tolerates some shade in summer).
- **Cultivation**: sow direct in spring and early autumn. Can be intercropped in summer between beans, peas or sweetcorn. Needs water in dry weather.
- **Sow/plant**: March–May/late August–September (outside); March/ September (under cover).
- **Spacing**: 15cm (6in) each way.
- **Harvest**: all year round, using different cultivars.
- **Pests and diseases**: slugs, birds (eat seedlings), downy mildew.

Key: ■ 4 (excellent)   ■ 3   ■ 2   ■ 1 (not so good)

SQUASH (WINTER) & PUMPKINS

In the same family as courgettes, pumpkins and hardier winter squashes provide an interesting and tasty crop into the autumn – one which suits perfectly the warming dishes of the cooling season. They are space-hungry, however. 'Bush' cultivars can be contained a little but more common 'trailing' varieties head off at great speed (and length) and need to be trained, even in big gardens.

- **Soil, position, climate**: reasonably fertile, well-drained soil.
- **Cultivation**: sow in pots or modules indoors or in a heated greenhouse in spring, or under cover in late spring. Harden off, then transplant when at three-leaf stage. Can be sown direct under cloches. Need watering and mulching. Train trailing varieties with pegs: in amongst sweetcorn works well. Cut wilting leaves at the end of the season to help the plants mature.
- **Sow/plant**: April–May (inside or heated greenhouse); May (under cover); June (direct, outside under cloches).
- **Spacing**: 90cm (35in) bush varieties; 1.5m (60in) trailing.
- **Harvest**: July–October. Leave on the plant as long as possible: they feel hard and sound hollow when mature. 'Cure' outside for 10 days to complete ripening and ensure long storage.
- **Pests and diseases**: slugs, downy mildew.

SWEDE

This hardy winter vegetable is best suited to those with larger gardens, because it grows slowly and takes up a bit of space. Swede likes cooler climates – hence its historic popularity in Scotland – and can stay in the ground in the winter and be stored thereafter, providing a very tasty and nutritious crop that suits the season's dishes well.

- **Soil, position, climate**: fertile, moisture-retentive soil. Doesn't mind the cold.
- **Cultivation**: sow outside in late spring. Needs regular watering in dry weather to stop roots becoming woody.
- **Sow/plant**: May (outside, cooler areas); late May–June (outside, warmer areas).
- **Spacing**: 90cm (35in) bush varieties; 1.5m (60in) trailing.
- **Harvest**: October–December (lift beyond December and store – see p. 126).
- **Pests and diseases**: slugs, downy mildew.

SWEETCORN

Freshness is more important with sweetcorn than with almost any other vegetable. It deteriorates rapidly after picking, so growing your own is the only way to experience it at its absolute best. Even though the plants grow to great heights (up to 2m/6ft), they can still work in smaller gardens, as long as you're content with a modest crop.

* **Soil, position, climate**: fertile, moisture-retentive soil, preferably on a sheltered site. Needs a warm summer to do well.
* **Cultivation**: sow in modules in late or direct in June (warmer areas). It is important to plant in blocks rather than rows, because sweetcorn is wind-pollinated. Planting through black plastic mulch, which warms the soil, speeds growth. To control weeds, hand weed to avoid damaging shallow roots.
* **Sow/plant**: April (under cover); May (outside, with cloches); June (outside, warmer areas).
* **Spacing**: 35cm (14in) each way.
* **Harvest**: August–October. Eat immediately.
* **Pests and diseases**: slugs, downy mildew.

Key: ■ 4 (excellent)   ■ 3   ■ 2   ■ I (not so good)

TOMATOES

If you only grow one thing … Tomatoes are relatively easy to grow, your own crop will taste infinitely better than almost anything you can buy, and the plants can thrive indoors, making them an edible crop suitable for the most space-constrained edible gardener.
A vast range of varieties is available and there are types to suit containers and pots as well as bigger spaces.

* **Soil, position, climate**: fertile, well-drained soil in a warm, sheltered, sunny spot. South-facing walls are good.
* **Cultivation**: start off indoors in modules then move into progressively bigger pots, hardening off when all danger of frost is passed. Can also start under cover. Cordon (or indeterminate) tomatoes grow tall and the side shoots must be 'pinched out'. These also need support. Bush or 'determinate' varieties are better for outdoor growing and there are dwarf varieties for containers. Plants in containers need careful, regular watering. Greenhouse growing extends season but can adversely affect flavour.
* **Sow/plant**: March–April (indoors or heated greenhouse); plant out May–June.
* **Spacing**: 45cm (18in) each way.
* **Harvest**: July–October.
* **Pests and diseases**: potato and tomato blight; slugs on mature fruit.

Key: Space Time Gourmet Season Hassle Beauty

TURNIPS

A close relative of the swede, turnips need not be the dull agricultural fodder crop of reputation. Small, tasty, fast-growing varieties are useful in smaller spaces and they can provide an extra crop from their leaves or 'tops'. Turnips suit cool climates and different varieties can provide an almost year-round supply.

- **Soil, position, climate**: fertile soil with plenty of organic matter on an open site.
- **Cultivation**: early, fast-growing cultivars can be sown under cover or outside in early–mid spring; maincrop varieties are sown direct later in the summer. Need regular watering in hot, dry weather to prevent bolting.
- **Sow/plant**: March–August (outside, depending on variety).
- **Spacing**: 15cm (6in) each way.
- **Harvest**: June–December (maincrops can be stored thereafter).
- **Pests and diseases**: potato and tomato blight, slugs.

Herbs

All herbs are viable in small spaces, priced ludicrously in supermarkets and of great value in the kitchen. Most can be bought as small plants (albeit at more expense than seeds) and most are very easy to look after. Many herbs tolerate poor soils. Here is a list with brief comments:

Basil	Great for south-facing windowsill, greenhouses.
Bay	Evergreen shrub, very low-maintenance. Protect from frost.
Borage	Easy to grow, self-seeds, good in fruit punches.
Coriander	Needs warmth and sunshine.
Dill	Self-seeds, great with fish.
Fennel	Attractive perennial, leaves, stems and seeds all used. Attracts insects.
Horseradish	Needs to be contained as it is very invasive.
Lavender	Attracts beneficial insects, drought tolerant, aromatic.
Marjoram	Hardy perennial shrub, low-maintenance.
Mint	Plant in containers as it is very invasive.
Parsley	Pick the heads regularly for a continuous supply.
Rosemary	Drought-tolerant evergreen. Needs pruning in spring.
Sage	Evergreen shrub, needs pruning in spring.
Thyme	Hardy, evergreen shrub. Likes poor, free-draining soil.

Key: 4 (excellent) 3 ▨ 2 ■ I (not so good)

Fruit

This is not an exhaustive list of fruit that can be grown in the British climate. It omits warmer-climate fruits such as grapes, figs and apricots that grow successfully only in certain parts of Britain, and focuses on those that will grow in most areas.

Tree fruit

Compared to vegetable growing, which – depending on how you approach it – can demand regular time and attention, growing fruit on trees is relatively easy. And, perhaps surprisingly, fruit trees can be grown in very small spaces or trained up and over walls and trellises to provide an edible framework or boundary in the garden.

It's getting started with fruit trees that's the tricky bit. You need to know a little bit about four subjects:

Rootstocks: fruit trees are usually grafted on to a 'rootstock' (the root of a compatible tree) which has a particular characteristic. This is done so that the height and productivity of the trees can, to an extent, be predetermined. Rootstocks are also said to make the trees sturdier and more resistant to disease. However, there is a school of thought that prefers 'own-root' trees, which have strong roots, take longer to crop but grow more vigorously. Examples of apple rootstocks include 'M27' (very dwarfing – to 1.8m/6ft) or MM106 (semi-dwarfing – to 5.5m/18ft). So choose your rootstock according to your space and preference. It is possible to buy trees with different varieties on the same rootstock (for diversity and successful pollination); and there are even 'fruit and nut' trees available.

Pollination: the reproductive habits of fruit trees are complex. Some can pollinate themselves (with the help of insects such as bees) but others need similar, compatible trees nearby in order to set fruit. So depending on the reproductive habits of the tree you buy, you may need to plant several trees, buy two varieties on the same rootstock, or have a neighbour with compatible trees.

Pruning: fruit trees need pruning, usually in winter, to create a tree shape that optimizes fruit production (and doesn't fall over). Pruning is best learnt by 'apprenticeship' – watching an expert at work – but can also be learnt from books and diagrams.

Training: fruit trees don't need big open spaces to grow successfully. Many can be trained against walls and over garden structures in flat 'fans', 'espaliers' (branches following horizontal wires) or 'cordons' (straight lines). This dramatically increases your fruit-growing options if your outside space is very limited: the lawn can be kept free for the kids and the walls can become an orchard.

Fruit trees should be bought and planted in autumn and winter.

Key: Space   Time   Gourmet   Season   Hassle   Beauty

APPLE AND CRABAPPLE

This quintessentially British fruit can be grown successfully in containers and small spaces as well as big orchards. Growing your own apples gives you access to the vast range of delicious varieties that are now so hard to get hold of in the shops. Crabapples are worth growing because they are rarely sold commercially, make great jelly and have superb spring blossom. Choose a self-fertile variety of apple if you only have room for one tree.

- **Soil, position, climate**: rich, well-drained soil; an altitude of less than 120m (400ft) is recommended.
- **Care**: hang up codling moth traps in spring; remove fallen fruitlets in the summer and leaves in the autumn to reduce chances of disease; prune in winter. Apply greasebands to control aphids. Control weeds around the tree with mulch in late spring; remove the mulch in the autumn.
- **Harvest**: July–November, depending on variety. Some later varieties store well.
- **Pests and diseases**: aphids, codling moth larvae, canker.

CHERRY

There are two types of cherry: sweet ones, which are eaten straight from the tree; and acid cherries, used in cooking. Acid cherries such as 'Morello' can handle cooler, shady spots and are a good use for a north-facing wall. Sweet cherries need the opposite spot: a sunny, south-facing wall is recommended.

- **Soil, position, climate**: rich, free-draining soil; lots of sun for sweet cherries.
- **Care**: prune in spring, net against birds when fruit sets. Need regular watering in dry periods. Keep 1m (3ft) weed-free area around the base of the tree.
- **Harvest**: June–August.
- **Pests and diseases**: birds, aphids, cherry blackfly.

ELDERBERRY

More bush or shrub than tree, elders are so prolific in the wild (at least in England and Wales) that it would seem daft to plant one. But they provide two crops – elderflower in the spring and elderberries in the late autumn – and as a native tree are great for wildlife. Elders are available commercially and provide a low-maintenance – if rather vigorous – edible tree.

MEDLAR

You'll rarely find medlars on the shelves; they're an unusual fruit, picked late in the season (November) then left to 'blet' (decay) for a few weeks until edible. Medlars can be eaten as a delicacy in their own right or made into jellies. The trees are attractive and a medlar tree extends your fruit-growing season as far as it can go in the British climate.

MULBERRY

Mulberries don't turn up in the shops either, because they are impossible to transport and need to be eaten straight off the tree. The trees are slow-growing and it will be up to a decade before you get a crop from a newly planted one. However, the fruits are superb, the trees crop for many years and provide good shade too.

* **Soil, position, climate**: free-draining, fertile soil. Frost-sensitive and need a warm and sheltered position.
* **Care**: prune in winter.
* **Harvest**: August–September.
* **Pests and diseases**: few problems.

PEAR

Pears are a little more hassle than apples in that they are less hardy, therefore less suited to cooler parts of the country. And the fruits don't store so well. Still, if you have good sunshine and shelter in your space, growing your own is the best way to get hold of a perfectly ripe pear. Pears respond well to being trained but do not work as well as apples in containers.

* **Soil, position, climate**: rich, free-draining soil; warm, sheltered location.
* **Care**: hang up codling moth traps in spring, apply greasebands to control aphids. Control weeds around the tree with mulch in late spring; remove the mulch in the autumn. Remove fallen fruit. Prune in winter.
* **Harvest**: August–December.
* **Pests and diseases**: aphids, codling moth larvae, canker.

Key: Space Time Gourmet Season Hassle Beauty

PLUM (AND RELATIVES)

Plums are a fine summer crop with a season that can be maximized by choosing different varieties. Gages tend to prefer warmer climates, whilst damsons and bullaces can be grown successfully further north. All types flower early and are therefore susceptible to late spring frosts.

- **Soil, position, climate**: rich, free-draining soil; avoid growing where cool springs are likely.
- **Care**: prune in spring after the last frost, unlike other fruit trees. Otherwise mulch in spring and remove mulch in autumn, protect against aphids, collect fallen fruit.
- **Harvest**: August–October.
- **Pests and diseases**: aphids, silver leaf, canker.

QUINCE

These trees are worth considering for their aromatic blossom and interesting fruit. Quince makes superb jellies, 'cheeses' and desserts. The trees are easy to grow and can be planted in containers as well as developing into large trees.

- **Soil, position, climate**: rich, free-draining soil; doesn't have a problem with frost.
- **Care**: prune in winter, mulch in spring and remove mulch in autumn.
- **Harvest**: November.
- **Pests and diseases**: few problems.

Key: 4 (excellent)  3 ■ 2 ■ 1 (not so good)

Berry and soft fruit

Berry fruit takes up less space than tree fruit and can always be grown in containers, making it an option for the space-constrained gardener. Birds can be a problem, however, and if you have the luxury of enough space for a fruit cage, it's a garden structure worth building.

BLACKBERRY

Is it worth growing blackberries? The reason they are so abundant in the wild is that they are rampantly invasive: your garden could quickly become a bramble patch. However, the fruits are superb; and carefully trained and tamed, blackberries can provide an abundant crop, to which you have exclusive access.

* **Soil, position, climate**: blackberries aren't fussy.
* **Care**: train regularly during the growing season.
* **Harvest**: July–October.
* **Pests and diseases**: few problems.

BLACKCURRANT

Most of Britain's commercial blackcurrants end up in Ribena, leaving little for the jam-makers and summer-pudding enthusiasts among us. A new bush takes around three years to come into full production, so your blackcurrant crop is a long-term prospect.

* **Soil, position, climate**: rich, free-draining soil.
* **Care**: feed with garden compost or manure every other year; mulch in spring with straw or hay. Prune in winter. Net against birds.
* **Harvest**: June–September.
* **Pests and diseases**: aphids, birds.

BLUEBERRY

Much touted as a 'super food' for their various nutritional benefits, blueberries will fit into most gardens, but with one important caveat: they need acid soil. For most of us, this means that container growing is the only option. Two or more bushes are recommended to achieve good cross-pollination and a full crop takes 5–6 years to develop.

* **Soil, position, climate**: damp, acid soil with a pH of 4–5.5.
* **Care**: mulch with composted bark or pine needles, water with rainwater (not tap water) and net against birds.
* **Harvest**: July–September.
* **Pests and diseases**: few problems.

GOOSEBERRY

Gooseberries are the first berry fruit of the British produce year and not always easy to find in the shops, so growing your own is worth consideration. They cook beautifully and their famous seasonal pairing with elderflower should not be missed. The plants are very hardy and can manage in shade, although berries without full sun will remain sharp in flavour. Like all berry fruits, they are well suited to small spaces.

* **Soil, position, climate**: rich, free-draining soil; suitable for cooler climates.
* **Care**: mulch in late spring with hay or straw; prune in winter and summer.
* **Harvest**: June–July.
* **Pests and diseases**: aphids, mildew, gooseberry sawfly larvae.

Key: ■ 4 (excellent)　■ 3　■ 2　■ 1 (not so good)

RASPBERRY

There's a long list of good reasons for growing raspberries. Here are just a few: they tolerate cool conditions and grow successfully almost anywhere in the country; the range of varieties gives you a potentially lengthy season; they crop abundantly and, most importantly, they are a gourmet delight either fresh or preserved. Autumn-fruiting varieties take up less space and will crop in the first year after planting; summer varieties will give fruit in the second year.

- **Soil, position, climate**: plenty of compost or well-rotted manure; will tolerate some shade and cool conditions.
- **Care**: always buy healthy stock; never plant where there has been cane fruit or strawberries in the last six years. Provide support for canes as they grow. Cut back canes that have fruited down to ground level after harvest.
- **Harvest**: June–October.
- **Pests and diseases**: aphids, raspberry beetle, birds, viruses.

RED AND WHITE CURRANTS

Related to blackcurrant, these fruits are an essential ingredient of summer pudding and make good astringent jellies: being high in pectin they also help other jams to set. They crop on branches that are two years old, so this should be borne in mind when buying plants.

- **Soil, position, climate**: rich, free-draining soil.
- **Care**: feed with garden compost or manure every other year; mulch in the spring with straw or hay. Prune in winter. Net against birds.
- **Harvest**: June–September.
- **Pests and diseases**: aphids, birds.

 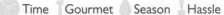

STRAWBERRY

The British strawberry industry is proud of the fact that, thanks to more and more high-tech growing methods, we now have a fresh strawberry season that stretches from March to December. But outside their natural summer season, strawberries taste tough and bland. Your own sun-kissed crop will provide a gourmet experience that far exceeds anything you can buy in the shops. Strawberries are ideal for small spaces and container growing and can provide a crop throughout the summer. They will provide a small crop in the first year, then be productive for around three years.

* **Soil, position, climate**: not too fussy about soil; slightly acid is OK. An open site in full sun is best.
* **Care**: plant pot-grown plants in autumn or spring. Strawberries send out stems that root to form new plants and most of these should be removed, leaving around three to create new plants. Strawberries need to be kept clean and dry so a mulch of black plastic or straw is recommended. The crop will need netting against birds. Start a new strawberry bed somewhere else after three years to avoid disease build-up.
* **Harvest**: June–September.
* **Pests and diseases**: birds, slugs, viruses.

Fruit and veg top five

Top five fruit and veg for the …

Complete novice, small garden	Complete novice, bigger garden	Gourmet	Aesthete	Self-sufficiency enthusiast
Garlic	Broad beans	Asparagus	Artichoke (globe)	Apples
Lettuce	Chard	Broccoli, sprouting	Beans (French)	Cabbage
Rocket	Leeks	Fennel	Crabapples	Carrots
Tomatoes	Kale	Quince	Kohlrabi	Onions
Strawberries	Raspberries	Sweetcorn	Medlar	Potatoes

Key: 4 (excellent) 3   2 ■ 1 (not so good)

Vegans and vegetarians, look away now. This chapter deals with raising different kinds of creatures for the food they can provide or produce. The 21st-Century Smallholder will, however, get much more than meat, eggs, milk and honey from his or her livestock. Bees will pollinate plants and improve fruit and vegetable yields; pigs will clear and fertilize ground for planting; chickens will eat pests and weed seeds; and ducks will eat your slugs.

RAISING YOUR OWN FOOD

Throughout history, sustainable agriculture has relied on a 'managed symbiosis' between farmed creatures and crop growing. And it is for precisely this reason that modern agriculture is unsustainable. Rather than coming from animals, fertility is often provided by fossil-fuel-dependent artificial fertilizers that give the crops a quick fix but don't build the fertility of the soil. And such is our appetite for meat in the Western world that two-thirds of our arable agriculture is given over to providing feed for animals. The planet cannot provide for this carnivorous appetite to be extended globally.

Perhaps we should all just give up meat and stop fantasizing about keeping our own chickens, pigs or bees? If we did eschew all animal products, however, organic agriculture would become unsustainable and smallholding impossible.

A fully self-sufficient smallholding of the type championed in John Seymour's *Complete Book of Self-Sufficiency* is a 'managed ecosystem', in which everything is recycled and animals are essential to build soil fertility. Take the pigs, cows and chickens out of the equation and fertility has to be imported from somewhere else: the smallholding loses its independence.

What you end up with in such 'closed-loop' farming, however, is, arguably, a perfect diet. It is no accident that the cuisine frequently touted as the world's healthiest – the peasant food of the Mediterranean – is rooted in small-scale, sustainable agriculture. A true smallholder is unlikely to eat too much meat, because the inputs needed to sustain, say, the levels of chicken or beef consumption common in the Western diet are impossible to produce on a self-sufficient smallholding. Try to keep chickens for food in an average suburban garden and you will probably have to recreate precisely the unpleasant, intensive conditions that put you off chicken in the first place.

It is extremely unlikely that a 21st-Century Smallholder is going to become completely self-sufficient. (If, however, you are interested in the implications and economics of this, read Chapter 7, 'Going all the way', for a practical introduction.) Growing food on balconies or in back gardens means that we will almost always have to 'import' fertility in the form of, say, manure from the local stables, or municipal or commercial compost. Most of us don't have enough space to grow the food to feed the animals so they can provide the fertility that ultimately feeds us.

And yet – assuming it is compatible with your beliefs – there is great value in considering raising your own food, albeit in a way that suits your circumstances. Bees and chickens, for example, will provide superb, healthy natural food in the form of honey and eggs whilst either pollinating or helping to fertilize your garden. And you don't need acres of outside space to keep them happy. For those lucky enough to have more space, pigs can provide great service to the 21st-Century Smallholder before providing great food; ducks can do slug patrol and goats provide home-made milk and cheese. And for those with the space and the inclination, there's even the possibility of a home supply of fish from sustainable aquaculture.

Bees

It is our duty to keep bees. In one of many examples of unfortunate human interference in natural systems, we imported a pest from Asia – the *varroa destructor* mite – that means honeybees can no longer survive in the wild in Britain. Because our bees have no defence against varroa, the only way to ensure a continuing supply of honey is to keep bees ourselves, managing both them and the pest. But bees are about a lot more than honey: they are central to our ecosystem, because many plants rely on pollination by bees in order to reproduce. As Albert Einstein is reported to have said, without bees, there is no life. It is also said that every third mouthful of food we eat depends on bees. Fortunately, there are many species of bee that can survive in the wild without human management (bumblebees, for example), but only *Apis mellifera*, the rather dowdy, small brown honeybee, can provide us with good supplies of honey as well.

But what is honey? Honeybees are social insects, living in complex and sophisticated communities. What distinguishes them from other bees is the fact that these communities are perennial, surviving from year to year rather than dying out in the winter. Key to their survival is honey, a food source gathered from the nectar of plants and processed within the bee into the delightfully sweet and sticky substance that is so good on toast. As well as being a great source of energy, honeybees' honey also stores indefinitely, so the overwintering colony has a valuable, non-perishable larder to keep it going until plants start to flower again in the spring.

Humankind has been exploiting this resource for around 5,000 years. Initially, we just took the honey from wild bees' nests. Although this resulted in the destruction of their home, it wasn't as bad for the bees as it sounds, because they could go and start a new nest somewhere else. The problem, of course, was guaranteeing a regular supply. 'Farming' bees – providing them with an ideal habitat (a hive) in return for a regular supply of honey – was the answer. The big advance in beekeeping was the introduction in the nineteenth century of movable frames within beehives that enabled honey to be removed – and the bees to be inspected – without destroying any part of the nest. Today, beekeeping is big business (for example, honeybees' value in North American crop pollination is estimated at $14 billion) as well as a productive pastime for the hobbyist or smallholder.

So is it worth having your own honey supply? It's not hard to get hold of high-quality honey these days; and while it isn't cheap, it's not something that tends to get consumed in large volumes. But there are some strong arguments for making (or, rather, letting your own bees make) your own. It's good for your garden: a honeybee colony contains tens of thousands of worker bees who will help pollinate your plants and food crops. If you have a sweet tooth, honey is a relatively healthy way to satisfy it, and can be used as a substitute for sugar in almost all cases.

The medicinal properties of honey have been known for millennia – it has antibacterial and antimicrobial qualities – but these are often lost in commercial honey production. Making your own (or giving the bees the optimum environment in which to make it for you) is the best way to guarantee that all the good bits stay in. The 'cappings' of wax that seal each cell of honey, for example, are most likely to contain traces of pollen and propolis (an adhesive substance produced by bees, with healing qualities). The pollen content of cappings and of unprocessed honey can help counter hayfever; for sufferers, eating locally produced honey is said to be the best way to build defences against local pollen.

And whilst the 21st-Century Smallholder is unlikely to strike it rich from honey production, it is one of the few foodstuffs in which you can rapidly become self-sufficient. A well-managed hive can produce 10–35 kilos (25–80lb) of honey each year, which will give you at least a jar a fortnight!

Finally, it's a satisfying pastime that – like growing your own food – brings you closer to the natural rhythms of the year.

Keeping bees – what it takes

Skill

As with so many aspects of being a 21st-Century Smallholder (or indeed a full-time smallholder), beekeeping is something best learnt by 'apprenticeship' to someone who knows what they are doing. You need to know quite a lot about bees and their habits in order to understand about honey production; and foreknowledge is essential before diving into a hive for the first time.

However, few of us have beekeeping friends or relatives living nearby and the days when households routinely had hives are, of course, long gone. The next best thing, then, is to join your local beekeeping association and get on a course. This will not only equip you with the essential background knowledge about bees and beekeeping: it will also introduce you to local beekeepers who will often be happy to help a novice along. See p. 218 for beekeeping organizations, contacts and background reading.

There's no 'innate' skill needed in beekeeping: everything you need to know can be learnt by observation and practice. However, a relaxed approach to the bees is always good. Working with the bees gently and restraining one's desire constantly to pester them is important and it is for this reason that women are said to make particularly good beekeepers.

It is also useful in beekeeping if you are not frightened of hammers and nails. You don't have to build the hives yourself – they can be bought ready-made (at extra cost) and second-hand ones will of course be already made up. However, making the hive yourself does save some money. I was assured by a supplier that this was a 'therapeutic' activity, something not reflected in my first swearing-laden attempt: there are scant instructions in a flat-packed beehive and all the measurements are imperial. However, it is ultimately very satisfying, not too tricky and, whatever happens, you are likely to have to build the frames (on which bees build honeycomb) yourself. So a bit of (very) basic woodworking skill is helpful.

Equipment

Beekeeping does involve a lot of gear. To get kitted out for your first colony will cost in the region of £300 if you are buying everything new, although most beekeeping requisites can be had second-hand on the Internet or through beekeeping associations. New beekeepers are, however, recommended to buy new hives to minimize the risk of disease. At a minimum, you will need:

- **Some bees**: these can be had for free during the swarming season, or you can buy a 'nucleus' of bees (a queen and some workers) from beekeeping suppliers or specialist beekeepers. The latter option gives a better guarantee of well-behaved and disease-free bees, but may add around £130 to your set-up costs.
- **Hive**: this is the single most expensive item and, ideally, you should ultimately have two in order to manage your bees more effectively (and get more honey). The traditional sloping-walled, white-painted beehive that we most readily think of is in fact the most expensive and least efficient. The WBC hive, as it is called, is heavy and has room for fewer bees and honey that the National hive, less visually alluring but most commonly used in Britain.
- **Hive tool**: a simple tool to prise apart the hive and remove frames, needed because the bees tend to glue everything together with propolis.
- **Smoker**: this pacifies the bees whilst you are working on the hive. The smoke triggers an ancient instinct, making the bees think there is a fire nearby: it causes them to gorge on honey (in readiness for an escape flight) so they become more placid.
- **Protective clothing**: opinions differ on this. Some recommend nothing less than an all-in-one bee suit for beginners, others are less prescriptive. The bare minimum is a veil: a sting on the face is not alluring and a sting in the eye can cause blindness. You can get away with standard overalls (but not blue ones, which bees apparently hate). Or just wear a jacket, long trousers and a pair of Marigolds and make sure everything is well tucked in.
- **Bee brush**: something that gently persuades the bees to get off whatever it is you want to look at. A long feather works well.

If you are building a hive, you will also need a ruler with imperial measurements, a decent hammer and a try square. To extract honey you will need a honey extractor, which removes the honey from the comb by centrifugal force. Even the simplest of these is costly (£100+), so the new beekeeper is recommended to borrow the use of one from a local beekeeping association or experienced beekeeper.

Resources

Bees are clever enough to get all their resources themselves, finding food and water wherever they are. However, if you take their honey in September, they will be left with little for the winter, so you will need to feed them with sugar solution in the autumn so they can build up stores to survive the cold months.

Space

You do not need a big garden to keep bees. The main problem is likely to be neighbours, who may not appreciate that bees are not particularly interested in stinging people, and that even if they do, their stings are largely preferable to those delivered by wasps, mosquitoes and horseflies. The trick is therefore to site the hive(s) discreetly if possible, perhaps building a simple 1.8m (6ft) mesh barrier around it so that the bees are forced to fly off above head height. Such a barrier may also be useful if there are children around, whose curiosity may be annoying for the bees and therefore distressing for the infants. Flat roofs and balconies are also ideal for bees (assuming they are not too exposed) and cities abound with discreet rooftop beekeepers.

Time

Beekeeping is not particularly time-consuming: there is virtually nothing to do during the winter apart from check that the bees have enough food and make sure the hive is OK; and during the peak season of May to July around six hours a month is the maximum you should need to dedicate. An important caveat is that a colony of bees is likely to swarm (duplicate itself) in May/June if the swarming process is not dealt with: although, paradoxically, they are at their most mellow when swarming, a big buzzing clump of thousands of bees can be very unsettling for neighbours. And if the swarm is not captured it may decide to go and live in someone's chimney. So planning for the swarming season – which involves careful observation of the bees and a strategy for managing the swarm – is an important consideration in beekeeping. May is probably not the best time for the unprepared beekeeper to go on holiday.

See also May (p. 150) in Chapter 5, 'The 21st-Century Smallholder's year planner'.

Money

Once the initial set-up costs are out of the way, the main cost in beekeeping is your time.

SET-UP COSTS (COSTS ARE ALL FOR NEW EQUIPMENT)	
Bees (if commercial nucleus bought):	£130
Hive, including frames + 2 supers (new):	£220
Second hive (not needed straight away, but recommended by year two):	£150
Smoker:	£30
Hive tool:	£10
Bee suit:	£70

Legal considerations, paperwork

There is no law to prevent you keeping bees on your own property; and by arrangement you may well be able to have additional hives in local parks or on allotments (where honeybees' pollination skills are always welcomed). Bees don't need any paperwork (unless they are being imported or exported). However, if you discover that your colony has varroa, or the more serious American Foul Brood or European Foul Brood diseases, then your nearest Bee Inspector from the National Bee Unit must be notified.

Chickens

Chickens provide the obvious entry into livestock for the 21st-Century Smallholder. They'll be happy in back gardens and, as well as producing a regular supply of eggs, will perform weeding, manuring and pest-control duties. Chicken-keeping is, however, worth it for the eggs alone. It's widely known now that 'free range' on an egg box means little more than the fact that there is a tiny door somewhere in the dingy barn in which thousands of such birds may be kept. Organic eggs mean a happier life for the chicken and a healthier egg for the consumer, but even most of these are not a patch on the real thing: a just-laid, still-warm egg heading to your kitchen from the henhouse. Eggs keep reasonably well, but the quality starts to decline as soon as they are laid. As with so many foods, the longer they spend on the road or in the shops, the less good they'll be to eat. The gastronomic argument for keeping your own supply is very strong indeed. You may have fewer eggs in the winter – or no eggs – depending on the breed of chicken you choose and whether you use artificial light. But maybe this becomes a seasonal event rather than a problem.

Could you also keep chickens to eat? Of course; but if you are an average British consumer of chicken, supplying your own needs will be a major undertaking. We eat around a third of our body weight in chicken each year. So a family of four could need as many as sixty-two chickens a year to feed their habit. Which is a serious flock (given that you'll also want eggs, breeding stock and a cockerel, which the neighbours won't like) and another indicator of the unsustainability of modern eating habits. For most people, eggs and maybe the odd older bird for the pot is probably the most practical chicken operation.

If you're getting into food-growing, chickens have a strong role to play. Using a movable chicken ark, they can be 'tractored' over ground that you want to prepare for sowing. They will scratch away at the ground, breaking it up a little, and, most importantly, will go pecking for weeds, weed seeds and pests, as well as applying a light dressing of nitrogen-rich fertilizer. So if you're a lazy 21st-Century Smallholder, chickens are a very good idea. Practitioners of permaculture, which seeks to create beneficial natural relationships to productive ends, take the chicken symbiosis thing one step further. They suggest building a combined 'chicken-greenhouse' in which the chickens keep the greenhouse warmer at night and the greenhouse warms up the chickens in the morning: if you have a good few chickens and a decent greenhouse, this might be worth a try.

And whilst it's difficult for most of us to get captivated by the personalities of bees, chickens can be much more alluring. Children can make friends with them; they can defuse (or detonate!) family rows; and they bring the fresh dimension of animal husbandry into your life.

It's not all a rosy bucolic glow with chickens, though. At the time of writing, a fox attacks our tiny new-laid lawn every night unless I use the celebrated and effective 'male urine' deterrent. I live in central London, in the middle of back-to-back terraced houses, all of which have chicken-free gardens with good-sized garden walls. The fact that Mr Fox is prepared to overcome all of this just to mess with our grass, when all around us are parks and fast-food outlets, suggests that there are more than a few of him in my street alone. Put some chickens in your garden and, wherever you live, particularly if it's in a city, the fox will come calling. Unless you assiduously lock the birds up at dusk and take them out at dawn, he'll have the lot. (He may even attack during the day.) So be prepared to lose a few; rats are a problem too.

Making chicken-keeping a little more complicated is the fact that not all chickens are the same. There are around a hundred breeds in the UK, each with their own characteristics and specialization. The broad choice is between hybrids, which are cheaper and offer higher egg yields (up to 300+ per year); and pure breeds, which are more expensive, lay fewer eggs (around 100 per year) but will be hardier and better at the alfresco scratching and foraging side of things. The easiest route for a 21st-Century Smallholder looking for an egg supply is to buy hens at 'point of lay', which means 16–18 weeks old and ready to start laying in around four weeks.

Some popular breeds:

PURE BREEDS	HYBRIDS
Welsummer	Black Rock
Cuckoo Maran	Calder Ranger (Columbian Blacktail)
Light Sussex	Speckledy
Rhode Island Red	White Star
White Leghorn	

Keeping chickens – what it takes

Skill

Chicken-keeping needs no specialist skills beyond an ability to empathize with other creatures. *Secret Life of Cows* author and organic farmer Rosamund Young points out that hens are inquisitive, playful and sociable. If you interact with them at feeding time they will come to see you as being at the head of the pecking order, which makes for a harmonious flock.

Equipment

Another reason for chickens' suitability to the 21st-Century Smallholder is that you don't need specialist equipment to keep them. Your chicken infrastructure could be anything from a home-made henhouse and chickenwire run, through to a top-of-the range poultry ark costing several hundred pounds. You will also need a feeder and a drinker; these can either be created with a bit of DIY or bought cheaply.

Resources

Food: chickens need a varied diet. Most require a 'compound feed' to meet their protein requirements and this will need to be organic if you are worried about GMOs potentially creeping into your food chain. Chickens will also get nutrients from grass and the soil and will benefit from the odd bit of grain. They need grit in order to digest properly and will also enjoy brassicas and greens to peck at.
Water: chickens need a constant supply of clean, fresh water.
Grass: this is what they most like to be on.
Wood shavings, sawdust or clean, chopped straw: to line nest boxes.

Space

What is the minimum space for a chicken? It depends on how 'free range' you want to be. Chickens can live in an ark that takes up only 2m x 1m (6.5ft x 3.25ft) of space; however, this will have to be moved around so that pests and diseases don't build up in the ground. So a grassy space twice this big could theoretically support a few chickens. More room is, however, preferable: ideally they should be able to run and stretch when outside the henhouse. But this still means that most gardens are viable for chicken-keeping. Grass is ideal: it provides them with extra nutrition and is their preferred surface. Bark chippings or similar can substitute if you have no grass. Chickens also need somewhere to have a dust bath.

Time

Chickens won't take up much of your time, but like any animal in your care, they are a tie. They need to be let out first thing and shut up at dusk, fed, watered, cleaned out regularly, talked to and maybe tractored around the garden. Although they can in theory be left to their own devices for a couple of days, ideally you will need friends or neighbours to look after them whenever you go away.

Money

Keeping chickens can be done on a shoestring budget, depending on how smart you want the birds and their housing to be.

SET-UP COSTS	
Chickens:	
Ex-battery layers:	25p each
Hybrids:	£5 each
Pure breeds:	£15–20 each
Housing:	
Home-made ark:	free
Basic wooden ark for a few hens:	£200
Posh wooden ark for 10+ chickens:	£300–500
Feeders/drinkers:	either home-made or £5–40 depending on materials
ONGOING COSTS	
Food:	roughly £12 per chicken per year for organic feed, less for non-organic

An honourable mention must go to the Eglu, a trendy plastic henhouse and run that can be bought complete with two hybrid layers, feed and all necessary equipment for £365.

Legal considerations, paperwork

Chickens are pretty much an admin-free zone. Small, movable chicken housing doesn't need planning permission, and there is no need to register a flock under 250 birds. The only time you are likely to encounter problems is if you keep a cockerel, which will inevitably upset nearby neighbours, or if local by-laws, deeds or tenancy agreements forbid chicken-keeping. Eggs can be sold to friends, from your house or at a market stall, but to retailers only if you are a registered producer.

Pigs

'The hogs are the great stay of the whole concern,' wrote William Cobbett in *Cottage Economy*, a handbook for 19th-Century Smallholders. Cobbett was referring not only to the ability of pigs to provide superb meat that could be preserved for the rest of the year as bacon and ham; but also to the value of their manure, which, when properly rotted down, is vastly superior to both horse and cow dung as a fertilizer. For these reasons pigs have long been central to smallholding life. But what value do they have to the 21st-Century Smallholder? Won't you simply be arrested for having one in your back garden?

The short answer is no (and a more detailed answer is on p. 113). It is possible to keep a pig, or even several pigs, at home. Should you choose to do so, then there is the potential to do anything from fattening some bought-in pigs to turn into pork or bacon for yourself or for sale, to breeding pigs for fun and profit. Pigs also have many uses before being abruptly transformed into delicacies. They are excellent rotovators, turning rough ground into something ready for planting whilst at the same time applying fine fertilizer to it. Properly managed, pigs – originally woodland creatures – have a fine symbiosis with orchards. In return for shade and food they provide fertility and clear up the windfalls. Pigs will also recycle all your vegetable and dairy waste.

And, of course, once they have completed these tasks, pigs provide an amazing range of fine meat. Your own will be better than almost anything commercially available. Intensively reared pigs have a short, nasty life and an unnatural diet; and the resulting meat – flabby, waterlogged and bland – reflects this. Really high-quality, rare-breed pork and bacon are completely different, a taste many of us will have almost forgotten. It's also a good deal more expensive than intensively reared meat, so what with all the other good things pigs can do – and the fine company they make – pigs can make financial as well as gastronomic sense as part of a 21st-Century Smallholder's set-up.

However, once you take on even one pig you enter the 21st-Century Smallholding 'big league'. Pigs need paperwork, veterinary care, lots of food and plenty of time and attention from their keepers.

Two types of pig-keeping:

Weaners for pork or bacon: pig-keeping doesn't have to be a year-round commitment. Fattening 'weaners' (eight-week-old pigs just weaned from their mothers) is the easiest route. Even slow-growing rare breeds are ready to be turned into succulent pork at twenty-six weeks, meaning that you need to devote only around four and a half months to keeping them and feeding them up. Keeping them for bacon takes longer – about ten months. Taking on two pigs as a minimum is often advised (as they love company) and if you can sell one and a half to family and friends and keep a half for yourself, you could even make a profit. And you'll also get free fertilizer and rotovation services and a fulfilling (if fleeting) relationship with intelligent and sociable creatures.

Pigs for breeding: moving up the scale of pig husbandry, you could get into small-scale pig breeding. There is a good demand for rare-breed weaners for fattening, so keeping a sow, who could produce two litters of at least ten piglets a year, would provide income as well as 'free' weaners. The downside is that this is a year-round commitment, and altogether more involved than merely fattening a pair of pigs.

Breeds of pig and their uses

'Rare breed' pigs are the best option for any smallholder because they are hardier and provide higher-quality meat. Each has its characteristics and its uses, summed up in the table below:

BREED	CHARACTERISTICS	USES
Tamworth	Red-haired, athletic, good 'rotovators'	'Dual purpose': pork and bacon
Gloucestershire Old Spot	Pink-white with distinctive black spots, good in orchards	Dual purpose
British Lop	Hardy, make good mothers, lop ears	Dual purpose
British Saddleback	Black with white saddle, hardy, make good mothers	Dual purpose
Oxford Sandy & Black *	Colours as in the name; hardy, docile, pleasant personality	Dual purpose
Large Black	Black, lop-eared	Bacon
Berkshire	Black with a white face, good temperament	Pork
Middle white	Hairy white pig with rather ugly flattened face	Pork

* Not a true rare breed.

Keeping pigs – what it takes

Skill

You do not need to be an expert livestock farmer to keep pigs: the skills needed are within reach of everyone. The key – as with all animal husbandry – is in keeping them happy. Pigs can grow to daunting sizes but it is said that only badly treated pigs behave badly: the rest, as long as they have good food, company, water and shelter, are very easy to be around. You will, however, need some awareness of the illnesses of pigs and a more in-depth knowledge of pig behaviour and biology is essential if you are going into breeding. It also helps to be able to administer injections, as pigs need to be wormed regularly and injections are the most reliable way of getting the drug into the beast.

Equipment

Getting set up for pig-keeping does need a bit of investment and thought. But most of the kit lasts a long time so pigs become cheaper over the years.

Housing: although most rare breeds are hardy and happy to be outside in all weathers, pigs need somewhere dry and warm to sleep. A wooden pig ark is the best option for the 21st-Century Smallholder: these are relatively cheap (or easy to build), don't need planning permission and can be moved around.

Fencing: pigs can cause chaos if they get into in the wrong places. Wire-net fencing with barbed wire at the bottom is ideal; electric fences also work and have the added advantage of being more easily movable.

Feeding and drinking troughs: these need to be very heavy or set into concrete so that the pigs don't knock them over: cheap alternatives are old butler's sinks or buckets set in cement.

Resources

Pigs get through a lot of resources. If you are trying to turn your garden or smallholding into an 'ecosystem' which manages itself with minimum input, then pigs are probably inappropriate because they need a lot of 'input' in the form of a good supply of high-protein, grain-based feed. Only the much larger smallholding is likely to be able to grow and process this sort of stuff itself.

Straw: pigs need a supply of dry straw for bedding. They never soil their bedding, but it is good to keep it clean and fresh.

Water: pigs drink a lot, so a supply near to where they feed is essential.

Food: a pig will get through 0.5kg (1lb) of pig nuts (grain-based pig food) per day for every month of their age up to a maximum of 3kg (6lb) a day. They will also need fruit and vegetables and, ideally, access to soil and grass, from which they extract vital nutrients.

Space
Whilst it is theoretically possible to keep pigs in poky urban gardens, in my view it is only really appropriate to keep them if you have a very generous outside space: a field, or a garden of, say, 300+ square metres. Pigs will simply trash a small garden (albeit in an ultimately constructive and fertile way) unless they are tightly confined; and doing that would defeat the object of rearing 'free-range' pork. Space for an ark or sty is essential and the ability to shift the fencing so that the pigs move around on the space (perhaps as part of a crop rotation) is ideal.

Time
Pigs need to be fed twice a day, in a visit that will inevitably take longer than the 10 minutes it needs. Pig-keeping is only a year-round tie if you are breeding; otherwise, rearing weaners for pork could be timed to fit around other commitments. So, for example, you could keep weaners and still go on holiday without needing other smallholders on standby.

Money*

Pigs:	£50–80 each
Housing:	£250+
Fencing:	£0–500
Troughs, bits and pieces of kit (if bought new):	£200
Food:	£100 per year (porkers); £200 per year (baconers)
Straw:	£30 per year
Vet:	£50 per year
Butchery:	£25 per pig

* This doesn't include the cost of the smallholder's labour, by far the biggest item if accounted for.

Legal considerations, paperwork
To keep pigs you need to apply for a CPH (County Parish Holding) number from your local Rural Development Service Office. If you are planning to keep them in a garden, then this may need to be assessed for suitability; and getting the neighbours on side, perhaps with the offer of a few juicy rashers, is recommended. You also need a herd number, which will be supplied along with the CPH number, which must be tagged or marked on pigs sent to slaughter or over twelve months of age. Joining the British Pig Association is essential if you want to sell your meat as 'rare breed' (which of course commands a price premium). You must also keep an Animal Medicine Record Book and complete an Animal Movement Licence whenever the pigs are moved. And you can't kill them at home: pigs need to be despatched at an approved abattoir.

Ducks

Domestic ducks fit nicely into the 21st-Century Smallholder's set-up. They produce good quantities of eggs, are superb at slug control and are themselves edible. Ducks are also hardier and less disease-prone than chickens. However, ducks have a complication that all aspirant domestic waterfowl-keepers should consider. They need a pond, which is fine, because every garden should have one. The problem is that garden ponds exist largely to promote biodiversity and encourage amphibians: and ducks will munch their way through most of the flora and fauna in a garden pond. So the first rule for integrating ducks into your food-producing ecosystem is to give them their own pond and also limit their access to the rest of the garden, otherwise they'll eat all your veg, too. Like chickens, their housing can be moved around the garden in rotation so they don't completely destroy the grassy surface they love. Also like chickens, ducks are prone to fox attack, so their housing needs to be made safe against this devious predator.

Your choice of duck is determined by what you are keeping them for. There are many types available – here is a short list of popular breeds:

Indian Runner – egg-laying, slug control
Khaki Campbell – egg-laying, slug control
Aylesbury – 'table' (eating)
Pekin – table
Rouen – table
Muscovy – table

Keeping ducks – what it takes

Skill
No need to take a degree in duck-keeping: they are relatively easy to look after. As with all animal husbandry, it's about their welfare and happiness.

Equipment
Ducks need similar accommodation to chickens, with a different door that takes into account their size and walking style. Fancy, bespoke stuff isn't necessary and home-made duck-housing will keep them perfectly happy. The pond is the main bit of 'equipment' needed for ducks: clean water is essential for them to keep their feathers in good condition and water is, of course, their favoured environment. A natural pond with a flow of water is ideal; however, ducks will be content with small, static ponds (made, say, from a small plastic tub) as long as they can get in and out

easily and the water is refreshed regularly. It is, however, only fair to give them the biggest, most natural pond possible.

Resources

Food: ducks need food to supplement what they will find whilst foraging, particularly in winter. They need a pelleted feed, and in winter will need fresh greens to make up for the lack of natural forage. Like chickens, they also need grit to aid digestion.

Water: ducks need a constant supply of clean, fresh water for drinking.

Grass: provides grazing as well as comfort.

Wood shavings, sawdust or clean, chopped straw: to line nest boxes.

Space

Confined to a small space, ducks will make a boggy mess of the ground they are on. A minimum recommended outside space per duck is around 2 square metres (6.5 square feet) and the ideal is about 4 (13). This is in addition to the space the pond and the duckhouse take up.

Time

As for chickens: ducks are quite low-maintenance. There is a minor difference in routine, in that ducks will lay eggs anywhere if left to their own devices. As they tend to lay at between 8 and 9 a.m. it is advised to wait until then before letting them out of their house for the day, so the business of egg-collection is made easier.

Money

Ducks:	
Hybrids:	£5 each
Pure breeds:	£15–20 each
Housing:	
Home-made house:	free
Basic wooden house for a few ducks:	£200
Food:	roughly £12 per duck per year for organic feed, less for non-organic

Legal considerations, paperwork

No hassles with ducks, as long as your pond doesn't abstract water in a big way or produce effluent, and as long as your duck-housing is not a large, permanent structure.

Fish

Can one be self-sufficient in fish? Is domestic aquaculture for food viable, affordable or ecologically sustainable? Despite the fact that fish farming is not something that the majority of 21st-Century Smallholders are likely to be inclined to undertake, it's worth a look for the interest value alone. After all, centuries ago, monasteries provided themselves with fish from ponds stocked with carp in a form of fish aquaculture which fitted into the rest of their agricultural practices. Despite the emergence of a few enlightened practitioners, modern fish farming is, in general, a ghastly business. Like other contemporary monocultures, it demands unsustainable inputs (pesticides, additives and the fact that it takes 3–5kg of wild or other fish to raise 1kg of farmed carnivorous fish such as salmon) and it creates unpleasant outputs in the form of pollution and animal cruelty.

However, there is another way. See a fish farm as an ecosystem, rather than a resource to be worked to exhaustion, and it is possible to create a sustainable supply of healthy food. Water is much more productive than land as a resource, particularly as a source of protein, because fish – being cold-blooded and supported by water – don't waste energy keeping warm or building big bone structures: they're mostly food. The trick is to make sure that this food can be produced in a way that is both economic and ecologically sound; and the key is to use herbivorous fish, which are highly efficient at converting food into flesh. As John Seymour points out in *The Complete Book of Self-Sufficiency*, carp can yield 1 ton per acre without feeding, given the right pond.

Keeping fish – what it takes

Skill
Sustainable fish farming involves a lot more than just feeding fish. It demands high levels of skill and understanding because you need to create a balanced ecosystem in which, for example, animal wastes are used to provide nutrients for creatures upon which the fish then feed. You also need to be an accomplished pond-builder.

Equipment
Surprisingly, ecological aquaculture doesn't demand much in the way of kit once the ponds are designed, built and stocked. If all has been done properly, the main piece of equipment you will need is a large net.

Resources

Food: If you're raising carnivorous fish such as trout, then they will need feeding. Even organic farmed trout – which feed on prawns introduced into watercress beds – need some supplementary protein and this will, of course, cost money. Vegetarian fish such as carp can get by with no feeding at all.

Water: goes without saying really: carp will manage in a pond but trout will demand a constant supply of fresh water from a stream to provide the oxygen levels and low temperatures they need.

Heat: common carp can manage without it but other carp species need a small heated pond in which to breed.

Space

This is the big one with aquaculture. Unless you're content with snacking on the odd goldfish, getting a serious amount of food from fish demands a big pond, or maybe a couple of big ponds that can be used in rotation. This means at least a spare 200 square metres (or about twice the size of an average British garden) just to keep the fish in. So aquaculture ideally suits those of us with a good amount of land.

Time

Assuming you're going for the low-maintenance common carp option, time input is likely to be minimal once the operation is established.

Money

The sums involved in domestic aquaculture will vary hugely depending on whether you have ponds or need to build them, and how low- or high-tech your approach to building them is. The fish themselves are not ruinously expensive: young carp can be had for less than £40 per hundred, although they then take several years to grow to edible age.

Legal considerations, paperwork

If your ponds abstract water or discharge effluents, then you will need to seek permissions from the Environment Agency; a permit is needed from the same organization to introduce fish into any body of water bigger than a garden pond.

Other livestock

Raising your own food works on a sort of sliding scale. It starts with bees, which need the least space and time, then moves on to chickens, which need at least a garden and daily attention. Then perhaps ducks, which have similar demands to chickens but also need a decent pond; and then pigs, easy to care for but requiring a generous outside space. Serious edible aquaculture, whilst very low-maintenance once established, demands even more space.

With the exception of aquaculture, these are the livestock options that are most practical for the 21st-Century Smallholder, who is looking to fit the growing and raising of food into a normal domestic situation. As long as you have a little time and money to spare and some space, ranging from a rooftop to a large garden, then some or all of the above could provide you with food, fulfilment and fertility to varying degrees. Move beyond bees, chickens, ducks and pigs, however, and you get inexorably closer to the world of real smallholding or even small farming. There will be people happy to keep, say, goats or sheep in small places; there are doubtless 'house cows' that live up to their name; but for most of us, getting more involved with livestock brings a commitment that probably won't fit easily into our lifestyles or, indeed, our gardens.

If your property includes several acres of land, however, then there are obvious arguments for going further with livestock. Cows will convert grass into milk, cream and butter whose quality will exceed anything you can buy and they provide fertility in the form of manure. Sheep will turn marginal land into fine meat. And a 'polyculture' of animals creates relationships that are beneficial for the land, the animals and thus the smallholder. Clearing woodland, for example, could be started by goats (which love woody stuff) and then continued by pigs, which will root and turn the soil. Cattle will graze the long grass, leaving the shorter stuff for sheep. And a combination of animals will help to reduce the build-up of pests and diseases. So for those 21st-Century Smallholders thinking about 'going all the way' (see Chapter 7), here's a brief summary of some of the issues involved in getting into more serious livestock.

Geese: their eggs taste good, and so does their meat; and they are additionally famed for their role as 'guard dogs'. But their size and the noise they make means geese are less compatible with 21st-Century Smallholding.

Goats: they're small and produce superb dairy products (goat's milk and cheese don't seem to provoke the same intolerances and allergies as cow's milk). Goats would seem the perfect choice for the 21st-Century Smallholder. It's their eating habits that let them down. If allowed, goats will rapidly lay waste to your edible (and ornamental) gardening efforts. As John Seymour, speaking of the goat enthusiast, puts it in *The Complete Book of Self-Sufficiency*: 'What he forgets about is that goats have 24 hours a day to plan to get into his garden, and he doesn't.' Your choices for restraint are either serious fencing, or tethering: which means either expense or a certain unkindness to an animal. Goats also need housing and, of course, milking.

Sheep: the main thing sheep bring to the party is their ability to graze on marginal land and turn its meagre output into high-quality meat as well as wool, enabling you to be self-sufficient in cardigans as well as protein. The reason sheep need more space than most 21st-Century Smallholders can provide is that they are

RAISING FOOD: SUMMARY

	Skill	Equipment	Resources	Space	Time	Money
Bees	2	2	1	1	1	2
Chickens	1	2	2	2	2	1
Pigs	1	2	3	3	3	2
Ducks	1	2	2	3	2	2
Fish	4	1	3	4	2	3
Geese	1	2	2	3	2	2
Goats	2	2	2	3	3	2
Sheep	2	2	2	4	2	2
Cows	4	3	4	4	4	4

Key: (four symbols) = lots   (one symbol) = minimum

susceptible to parasites that build up in the soil and are therefore best rotated with other animals. Also – and this applies to geese too – the ease with which you can buy superb organic and free-range produce (and thus encourage better agriculture) outweighs the hassle of growing your own in most situations.

Cows: there is a school of thought that says pasteurization removes much of the goodness from milk and may be at the heart of some of the health problems (such as intolerance) ascribed to dairy products. With 'green-top' (unpasteurized) milk hard to get hold of and under assault from legislators who would have its sale banned completely, a 'house cow' is the best way to get your own supply. This is just one of the many reasons for keeping cows: but this level of animal husbandry requires a very great deal of commitment. Cows must have a calf in order to produce milk, need careful and copious winter feeding, daily milking, much paperwork and lots of space for grazing. Only for the committed smallholder with plenty of land.

Legal, Admin.	Comments
🪶	The easiest way into raising food. Need some expertise and apprenticeship and maybe a few hundred quid to set up.
🪶	Cheap, easy, useful and happy in all but the smallest gardens. Need daily, year-round attention, though.
🪶🪶🪶	Very useful and productive, but for big gardens only. Daily attention essential, as is (some) paperwork. Not expensive to keep, but need housing, feeding and fencing.
🪶	Need similar attention to chickens, but also require a dedicated pond, so a bigger overall space is best.
🪶🪶	Vast outside space needed to accommodate worthwhile aquaculture. Low-maintenance once set up, though.
🪶	Noisy and bad-tempered. How much goose do you want to eat?
🪶🪶	Useful, but hard to contain destructive eating habits.
🪶🪶	Best if you have your own hillside.
🪶🪶🪶🪶	The centrepiece of a self-sufficient smallholding, but exact a heavy price in time and effort.

It's all very well growing and raising all this food, but what happens when it's ready? Many crops can be picked through a long growing season: winter leeks and cabbages, for example, will stay in the ground until you want them, and salads can be picked for the leaves if they are 'cut-and-come-again' varieties, or as whole plants over a long period if you sow in succession (see p. 54). Some crops will, however, present you with a glut, providing you with a big yield in a short season. There would be no point in growing just enough tomatoes or potatoes to eat when they are ready: you wouldn't be eating them for very long and it would be a criminal waste of a lot of growing effort!

GETTING
THE MOST FROM YOUR
HOME
HARVEST

Complete your first, tentative fruit- and vegetable-growing season and the remarkable skills of our peasant forebears become apparent. You need not only to be able to plan, sow and manage crops, but also to know how to deal effectively with the surplus your efforts inevitably create. Our ancestors mastered both of these out of necessity, creating a year-round food supply with no recourse to freezers, high technology or air-freighting. And the same applies to (some of) your livestock activities. You've killed your pigs – so now what?

Unless you 'go all the way' to a life of fully self-sufficient smallholding, you are never going to be dependent on your own stored or preserved produce for survival. Professional farmers and growers take care of this for us, ensuring that there is always something available. But there's little point in getting into growing and raising your own food if you're not also going to consider how to spin out your harvest. Not for survival, but for the sheer pleasure of having your own stuff available for as long as possible. And also for pride: there's nothing worse than watching all that effort of sowing, propagating, potting, planting out, protecting, feeding, watering and harvesting disappear in a mushy, rotting mess. It's a lot of work if all you get for your efforts is some extra compost!

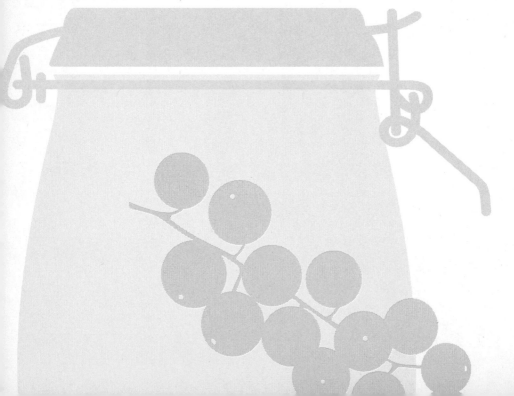

Storing and preserving fruit and vegetables

Although careful planning and sowing can provide a near year-round harvest for pretty much all fruit and for many vegetables, the harvest is over quickly. If you are growing on an allotment or large-garden scale, there may simply be too much to eat.

What you do with your cornucopia depends on what it is. Different produce responds to different treatments – and some things just need to be eaten. The table below gives a (slightly subjective) summary of this and may also help in planning your edible-gardening year.

For example, it illustrates that there's no need to be worried about a cabbage glut: not only do most cabbages stay happily in the ground until you are ready to eat them, they can also be stored, or pickled (say, as sauerkraut or the fiery Korean staple kimchi). On the other hand, an excess of sweetcorn should be the subject of a large barbecue or party. Sweetcorn can be dried and stored, but the real pleasure is in cooking the sun-kissed cob as soon as it has been picked.

	FRUIT	VEG
Stores well	Apples, Pears (not early varieties)	Beetroot, Cabbage, Carrot, Garlic, Kohlrabi, Onion, Parsnip, Potato, Pumpkin, Swede, Turnip
Good for bottling	All fruits	Tomato
Makes delightful things (e.g. pickles, preserves, wine*)	All fruits	Aubergine, Cabbage, Cauliflower, Courgette, Cucumber, Onion, Tomato
Can be dried	Apples, Damsons, Plums	Beans, Peas, Tomato
Freezes well	Berry fruits, Apples and Pears (if puréed)	Broad beans, Broccoli, Calabrese, French beans, Peas, Runner beans
Lasts well on the plant or in the ground	Rhubarb	Artichoke (Jerusalem), Beetroot, Broccoli (sprouting), Brussels sprouts, Cabbage, Carrot, Cauliflower, Celeriac, Celery, Chard, Chicory, Kale, Leeks, Lettuce and Salads, Parsnip, Swede, Turnip
Eat when ready: few or no good storage or preservation options		Artichoke (globe), Asparagus, Cardoon, Radish, Sweetcorn

* Almost any fruit or vegetable can be turned into wine. Parsnip, anyone?

Storage

A problem with many traditional ways of preserving the harvest is that techniques like bottling, pickling and drying take a bit of time and effort. Storage, on the other hand, is much easier, but it does demand that you have some space and the right kind of environment to keep your produce happy. Start thinking about where to put all those apples or onions and you rapidly realize that most houses were not designed with long-term vegetable storage in mind.

Ideally, you need somewhere dark, well ventilated and with a reasonably cool and constant temperature. Owners of cellars or large pantries are in luck. Attics are OK, but only during the coldest months because they are prone to heating up too much. Otherwise it is possible to build some storage space if you have the room outside. At the simplest level this could be a clamp (see below). Or if you have more space, time and a bit of budget, a shed or, even better, a modest straw-bale outbuilding (secured against mice and rats) could be the thing. If there's nowhere cool and dark in the house, then it's probably best to look to more labour-intensive (but very rewarding) ways of spinning out your harvest, such as bottling or preserving.

The key to good storage is to make sure your crops are unblemished and disease-free before being laid down. Many will last until early spring before the desire to rot or sprout finally takes over.

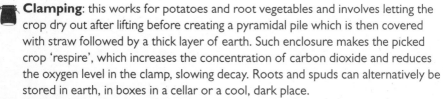

Clamping: this works for potatoes and root vegetables and involves letting the crop dry out after lifting before creating a pyramidal pile which is then covered with straw followed by a thick layer of earth. Such enclosure makes the picked crop 'respire', which increases the concentration of carbon dioxide and reduces the oxygen level in the clamp, slowing decay. Roots and spuds can alternatively be stored in earth, in boxes in a cellar or a cool, dark place.

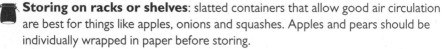

Storing on racks or shelves: slatted containers that allow good air circulation are best for things like apples, onions and squashes. Apples and pears should be individually wrapped in paper before storing.

Bottling

This needs some equipment but is worth considering if you simply don't have the time or energy to make vast quantities of jam or chutney or don't have a big freezer. Bottling involves sterilizing the produce by cooking it in sealed jars from which air is also expelled by the process to create a vacuum. All fruit can be bottled; and tomatoes bottle particularly well. If vegetables are to be bottled it should be in a pressure cooker, which really does sound too complicated to bother with. To do bottling you will need:

- 'Kilner' or equivalent thick glass storage jars with rubber seals and tight-fitting lids.
- A sterilizer or large pan (like a preserving pan) in which the jars can be boiled.

The process involves boiling the (sterilized) jars of prepared produce for a specific period of time. It is quite labour-intensive; and many with good-sized freezers will probably use them instead. However, if you have lots of shelves, lots of produce and don't fancy freezing, bottling is a practical (and good-looking) option.

Making delightful things

Before the advent of canning and freezers, we had to be inventive about storing food. And the big difference between modern and traditional methods is that the latter often transformed food into something new. Jams, chutneys, pickles (and even wine) not only preserve your harvest for years to come: they create delightful things in their own right. And there's no neighbourhood currency like a good jar of your own jam or chutney, or a bottle of successful country wine. Bookshops and the internet are overflowing with jam- and wine-making guides, so here is just a brief overview:

Pickling: this preserves food by using acid to prevent the enzyme action that spoils food. In chutneys and pickles, vinegar is the active agent, whilst in, say, sauerkraut, fermentation by lactic acid-producing bacteria works on the enzymes. Both methods are easy; but the products (and smells) of the latter are not to everyone's taste.

Jams and jellies: these work by cooking the food to destroy enzymes; the sugar stops the work of bacteria and other micro-organisms.

Wine: wines (and cider and perry) are fine homes for seasonal surpluses – the alcohol does the job of preserving.

Making pickles and jam is an easy, satisfying ritual that fills the house with seasonal smells and the shelves with long-lasting produce. It's not particularly cost-effective, as both products are commercially cheap to buy and you'll need a lot of sugar and a bit of time to make your own; but your own is somehow always best. Wine-making is a slightly bigger commitment, needing a minor investment in demijohns and fermentation locks, but simple country wines are easy to make.

Drying

This is a technique that used to sustain peasant Britain many hundreds of years ago: dried peas were what kept the people going through the winter. Is it worth it today? The legumes (beans and peas) that store so well are also at best when utterly fresh, and it seems a lot of effort to dry them unless it is a matter of survival or hard-core gourmet behaviour. Apples, cored and sliced, can be strung up over heat until crisp and dry, whereafter they will store well and taste great. You can even make your own prunes or sun-dried tomatoes, although the temptation of fresh produce and fine jams and pickles seems to me at least to outweigh the hassle involved.

Freezing

Smallholding purists may eschew the freezer on financial, philosophical and ecological grounds; but the fact is that most of us have one and they are very effective at preserving some fruit and veg, crucially with most of their nutrients intact. And I bet our ancestors would have jumped at the possibility of raspberries in the depths of winter. Beyond the purist's concerns, there are a couple of other issues with freezing: there isn't much room in many freezers and, also, some are prone to breaking down. But if you have a big, reliable freezer and a huge berry-fruit harvest, for example, it's hard to resist stocking up for winter. Some tips for freezing:

- Blanch vegetables first in boiling water for 1–2 minutes to destroy enzymes.
- Freeze separated fruit and veg on a tray first to stop them forming a solid block, then transfer to bags or tubs.
- Use well-sealed bags and tubs to avoid 'freezer burn'.
- Purée orchard fruits before freezing.

Preserving livestock

The vast majority of 21st-Century Smallholders will not be concerned with how to store or preserve their livestock. If you are lucky enough to have enough chickens to be able to eat the odd one, then you'll probably want to eat it straight away. Ditto ducks; and any fish farmers among us will be able to take what they need, when they want it. No need to worry about curing carp.

Pigs are where you will need to worry about storage and preserving. Kill a pig and you get enough meat to last a long time (up to 74kg/165lb for a 'baconer'). If it's a porker (grown for fresh meat rather than bacon) then there's no complication: once slaughtered and butchered, the animal goes straight into the (big) freezer, giving you a long-term supply of home-grown meat.

If, however, you've raised your pigs for bacon, then there is work to do. This was the traditional smallholding practice in the days before freezers: pigs were fattened through the year and then slaughtered in November, providing fleeting treats of black pudding, offal and pork before the bulk of the animal was turned into bacon and ham to last through the winter and beyond. Learn about the ghastly industrial process in which the majority of bacon and ham is produced these days and you will be highly motivated either to seek out traditionally prepared meat or even to grow and prepare your own. Preservation techniques for pork include:

- **Dry-curing**: traditionally used for bacon, this involves rubbing a salt/sugar mix into the meat repeatedly, over a period of up to three weeks, depending on the size of the cut. The salt and sugar suppress enzyme action and bacterial activity. The resulting bacon must then be hung in a cool, dry place and can additionally be smoked (see below).
- **Brine-curing**: hams can be cured by being submerged in a brine solution, then hung as for bacon before the optional smoking.
- **Air-drying**: more commonly associated with continental Europe, for hams this involves salt-curing then lengthy hanging (up to six months) in a cool and well-ventilated space. For salami-style sausages, salt is mixed with the meat mixture then the sausages are hung for a minimum of a month (but can also be eaten raw).
- **'Cold'-smoking**: this alone doesn't preserve the meat; it simply adds an antiseptic coating to it, as well, of course, as creating excellent flavour. So smoking is a technique that can be used in addition to any of the others. To do it yourself, you will need to build a smoker (perhaps above a stove or fireplace): this is a box big enough for the meat (or fish) into which smoke is diverted. If you have a large fireplace and high, wide chimney, then you could hang it in there and smoke it the

old-fashioned way. The temperature must be less than 50°C to stop the meat cooking, and the fire needs to be going for about a week.

STORAGE AND PRESERVATION SUMMARY

	TIME	SPACE	SKILL	KIT
Storage	▮	▮▮▮▮	▮	▮▮
Bottling	▮▮▮	▮▮	▮▮	▮▮▮
Making delightful things	▮▮▮	▮▮	▮▮	▮▮▮
Drying	▮▮	▮▮	▮	▮
Freezing	▮	▮▮	▮	▮
Curing meat	▮▮▮▮	▮▮▮▮	▮▮▮	▮
Air-drying meat	▮▮▮▮	▮▮▮	▮▮▮	▮▮
Cold-smoking meat	▮▮▮	▮▮▮▮	▮▮	▮▮▮▮

▮▮▮▮ = lots   ▮ = not much

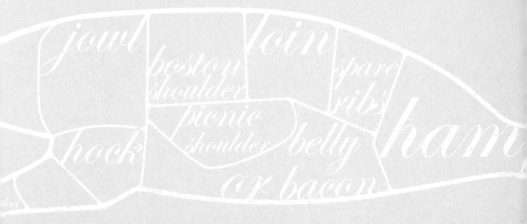

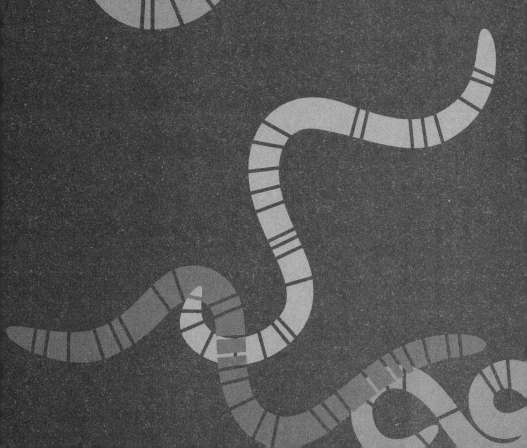

BUILDING
BIODIVERSITY

'Gardens are England's most important nature reserve'

Professor Kevin Gaston and Dr Ken Thompson, University of Sheffield

It is now over forty years since Rachel Carson wrote *Silent Spring*, a seminal book which first drew the world's attention to the destructiveness of industrial agriculture and, in doing so, kick-started the modern environmental movement. If we had heeded Carson's warnings, the British countryside would today be a very different place, bustling with a vast variety of wildlife. As it is, the agricultural heartlands of Britain are little more than a desert of monocultural, intensive food production. Look at the arable fields as you pass through these places in the growing season and most sport the tell-tale 'tramlines' used by boom sprayers to deliver herbicides, pesticides and fungicides to the crops. The popular image of the countryside – a gentle arcadia of small farms, swathed in flowers and buzzing with life – exists only in memory and in tiny pockets of Britain.

The industrialization of farming since the Second World War has had many consequences: it has given us food with potentially harmful residues, degraded our topsoil, polluted watercourses and transformed once-attractive rural Britain into an identikit wasteland of vast, prairie fields. But most of all, it has been largely responsible for decimating the country's biodiversity. Farmland species such as hare and partridge have declined by up to 85 per cent since the Second World War. As many as 54 per cent of our native bird species and 28 per cent of native plant species have declined in the last forty years. Tree sparrows are down by 89 per cent in the past twenty-five years; skylarks down by 58 per cent. Since the 1930s, 97 per cent of semi-natural lowland grassland (the flower meadows of our rural imaginings) has gone. I could go on.

Industrial farming affects species because it destroys or disrupts ecosystems. Herbicides kill the weeds on which many insects thrive. Insects that survive are killed by pesticides. As a result, birds and creatures further up the food chain have nothing to eat. Even if there was any food left for them, there's nowhere for birds and mammals to live in intensively cultivated fields without hedgerows or wild boundaries. And the flower meadows? Chemical fertilizers have largely turned these into monocultures, dominated by a single species of grass that crowds out all the others.

So how is the 21st-Century Smallholder's garden going to change all this? It can't, of course, have a direct effect. For the decline in the countryside's biodiversity to be properly reversed, agriculture has to change. And in my view this doesn't mean 'sticking-plaster' solutions like leaving little strips of uncultivated land at the edge of the farmland deserts for supposedly grateful creatures to live in. Doesn't that sound a bit like decimating an indigenous population and forcing the survivors to live in reservations? I thought we'd stopped doing that. I personally believe that Britain could feed itself (as it has before) with a more ecologically benign agriculture based on local production and consumption, mixed farming and organic principles.

But until the agricultural revolution happens – which it surely must, because apart from being highly destructive, today's practices are entirely dependent on oil – biodiversity begins at home, as the quote at the beginning of this chapter implies. Covering a total of one million acres, Britain's gardens are a final refuge for some of the creatures driven from the countryside. Our gardens, balconies and backyards can't provide a haven for everything: hare and partridge, for example, require much larger ecosystems. But they can still be home to an astounding variety of wildlife, from the microscopic to the big and furry.

There are reasons for doing something about biodiversity beyond just being nice to species under pressure and helping to counter the depredations of industrial farming. A garden (or even just a balcony) designed to attract wildlife is a beautiful place to be. There's deep satisfaction in observing the fruits of your labours: following birds through the nesting season or knowing that the frogs in the pond you built are on slug patrol tonight. Finally – and crucially for the 21st-Century Smallholder – building biodiversity is great for your edible gardening efforts. A garden with the right balance of bugs and creatures is less likely to suffer pest problems than an intensive food-producing space in which there's only room for crops.

How to design for biodiversity

It isn't hard to attract wildlife to your garden. Abandon it completely to nature and it will provide cover, habitat and food for wild species as the grasses grow and the brambles invade. Leave a big enough garden for long enough and you could end up with woodland. But in a completely wild state, your garden or outside space won't necessarily have too much room for its human occupants. And whilst you can make a food-producing 'forest garden', the untended wild garden is unlikely to yield as much edible stuff as you might like.

If you manage your garden according to organic principles, then biodiversity will automatically be boosted because a good mix of species is essential to pest control. A combination of laziness and lack of pesticides has turned my allotment plot into a nature reserve. Ironically, destroying biodiversity takes the most effort; an effort that must be sustained in order to resist the relentless fight back of nature. Bare-soil, chemical vegetable cultivation combined with a neatly clipped lawn and ultra-tidy flower beds will certainly keep the bugs at bay. The problem, of course, is that such an approach just creates more work, and more of the wrong sort of bugs: spray an infestation of pests and chances are that next year they will come back redoubled in force because the spray will also have killed their predators. Once you've started down the 'adversarial', man-vs.-nature garden path, the struggle is constant.

Gardening for biodiversity does, however, present the 21st-Century Smallholder with a dilemma. It can be tempting to think of every bit of outside space as somewhere to grow food. However, treating the whole space as nothing more than a market garden can mean neglecting creatures that might make the process of growing food easier. And missing out on the 'wildlife' bit arguably reduces the aesthetic appeal of your outside space too. As Patrick Whitefield says in *The Earth Care Manual*, 'Anything which adds diversity is likely to add to the health of the garden and to the aesthetic enjoyment of its human inhabitants.'

So the key is to try to strike a balance between the three main functions of a garden or outside space: recreation, food production and providing a haven for wildlife. The good news is that the wildlife side of things is easy, needn't take up too much space and is entirely complementary to the other two.

Creating a biodiverse outside space is all about providing both food and shelter for insects, birds, mammals and invertebrates and you can achieve this through a combination of planting and landscaping. In *How to Make a Wildlife Garden*, author Chris Baines notes that many of our native flora and fauna originally lived in a woodland environment and that a 'woodland glade' – with a balance between shaded and open space and a rich variety of habitats – is a good analogy for what an outside space built for biodiversity should be aiming to emulate. So here are five steps towards turning your outside space into a wildlife haven.

1. Be untidy

This is the easiest bit of all. I haven't yet met the people who live downstairs on the north side of my house, partly because they never use their garden. If they did, in high summer they would need a machete to get from one side to the other. The main 6 x 4.5-metre space contains a fantastic variety of flora: buddleia, bramble, elder, thistles, to name but a few. Two doors to the south in a similarly unvisited garden, a sycamore is growing fast and, in summer, foxgloves reach for the sky. Unwittingly, my neighbours are providing excellent habitat and food for inner-city wildlife. Their approach is a little too untidy for most; and a completely unmanaged space won't always develop a great diversity of species. But as a general rule, a garden or outside space will develop much more biodiversity if we resist the urge to, say, tidy up piles of wood or mow all the lawn to within an inch of its life at all times.

Untidiness tips:

- **Don't burn or throw away old logs and prunings:** piled up in a shady corner they will provide refuge for insects that will feed birds, solitary bees and wasps that will control pests and pollinate your plants, and small mammals like mice, voles and hedgehogs.
- **If you have a lawn, take a more relaxed attitude to mowing:** a closely mown lawn may be good for croquet but it doesn't provide much in the way of habitat or floral diversity. Either mowing less frequently, or using a strimmer or even a scythe instead of the mower will allow plants to flower and more insects to live in the lawn. Even better for wildlife of all kinds is to create a meadow: but this takes a bit of management (see p. 141).
- **Let things go to seed:** dead stems and seedheads provide habitat for bugs.
- **Leave the soil alone:** disturbing the ground under plants can disrupt the habitats of useful insects like mining bees.

2. Build a pond

Every outside space or garden should have a pond if possible. It needn't be big: a pond little bigger than a bucket can provide a useful habitat for all sorts of creatures. For the 21st-Century Smallholder's food-producing activities, a pond holds out the promise of an answer to every edibles gardener's prayer: slug control. Even the smallest ponds can attract frogs: and frogs love to eat slugs. Beyond amphibians, a pressured class of creature for whom garden ponds are an essential habitat today, ponds can attract fascinating insects like damselflies and dragonflies, give birds somewhere to bathe and the insects that hover over their surface provide food for birds and bats. And if you keep honeybees (see pp. 100–105) a pond will provide them with valuable drinking water: a single hive can get through 25 litres in a year.

Ponds can also play host to the ultimate slug controller, ducks (see pp. 114–15), but these will eat the frogs and pretty much everything else in the pond before starting on your vegetable patch. So to keep everyone happy, ducks ideally need a separate, fenced-off pond, making them a practical proposition only for those with a larger garden or maybe serious aquaculture aspirations (see pp. 117–18).

Pond tips:

- **Make your pond in the spring:** this is the best time to stock it with plants and frogspawn.
- **Site it in a sunny spot, away from trees:** leaves falling on a pond are not only a pain to clear, they also remove oxygen from it and create a foul-smelling layer at the bottom. Pond creatures also tend to prefer direct sunlight.
- **Give it shallow, sloping edges and a maximum depth of at least 60cm:** the shallows make a good birdbath, provide space for marginal plants and the slope makes it easier for the pond's larger inhabitants to get in and out. The depth stops it freezing solid in winter.
- **Use a pond liner:** if you have clay soil, you can create an impermeable base for the pond by 'puddling' it with plenty of energetic stamping. Otherwise, a butyl rubber pond liner gives the maximum flexibility, because pre-formed plastic or fibreglass pond liners rarely give the shallow edges that amphibians need. The base of the pond should be free of sharp stones and lined with sand or damp cardboard before the liner goes in. A layer of sandy soil on top then provides somewhere for plants to root. Make sure the liner isn't exposed when the pond is full, as sunlight can damage it.
- **Fill and top it up with rainwater if possible:** whilst you can get rid of the chlorine in tap water by leaving it to stand for a while, it's not possible to remove its often high mineral content, which can lead to excessive build-ups of algae. Rainwater is better, but in short supply when it's most needed in the summer. All of which is another good argument for serious rainwater harvesting (see p. 186).
- **Add a bucketful of water from an existing pond:** this will contain eggs, spores and seeds that will help creatures to colonize your pond.
- **Stock it quickly with oxygenating plants:** small ponds may not naturally be colonized by the right plants quickly enough, so a trip to the garden centre or a friend's pond will be necessary. Water milfoil and water starwort are well-known native oxygenators. Otherwise, the pond should have a mixture of submerged plants, 'emergents' that grow in the shallows and floating plants such as water lilies. You may need initially to 'anchor' submerged plants with stones to stop them floating to the surface.
- **Avoid fish:** they will eat the amphibians, ruining your slug-control plans.
- **Keep an eye on it:** whilst a golden rule of wildlife gardening is minimum interference, the pond will need some maintenance: to shift excessive algae, maintain the water level or maybe remove duckweed so there is always some clear water showing.

3. Plant natural habitats

A little untidiness and a pond create incredibly rich habitats. But there are many more steps you can take towards providing shelter for creatures that will make the garden lovely and keep the vegetable pests at bay.

Habitat-planting tips:

- **Go for 'maximum edge':** the point where one ecosystem meets another is often the most productive – estuaries or the edges of woodland, for example, are extremely biodiverse. A garden, usually bordered on three sides, is ideal for achieving 'edge'. Low-growing shrubs can provide shelter and food for wildlife and be planted in front of trees, which provide yet more habitat. This 'multi-level' approach suits a broader range of fauna: for example, blue tits prefer to forage higher up than great tits. Hedges are also superb wildlife habitats.
- **Plant native trees and shrubs:** these are often considered best as they support more insect species and are less likely to be uncontrollably invasive. Hawthorn, for example, supports over two hundred insect species whilst sycamore manages only forty-three. Mulching between the shrubs whilst they grow will suppress weeds.
  - **Some useful native shrubs for gardens:** wild roses, elder, honeysuckle, holly, bramble.
  - **Some useful native trees for gardens:** crabapple, silver birch, hawthorn, rowan.

◉ **Make a meadow:** you won't find idyllic wildflower meadows in the countryside
› any more, so why not make one at home? If you have enough space, allowing the
grass to grow tall and possibly seeding it with wildflowers will attract butterflies,
small mammals and, as a result, maybe even birds of prey. Meadow essentials:

◉ **Planting** – it is unlikely that wildflower seeds will survive the competition
of the grass in an established lawn, so they ideally need to be in 'plugs' that
enable them to survive until germination. A more labour-intensive alternative
is to strip the existing turf and sow a mixture of grass and flower seeds on it.

◉ **Mowing** – meadows are not entirely 'natural': it is annual cutting that
allows the wildflowers to flourish. So a late-summer/autumn mowing is all a
meadow needs. The lawnmower will not be up to this task: it's strimmer or
scythe, depending on your attitude to manual labour, fossil fuels, etc. Remove
the mown grass, otherwise the soil will gain fertility and favour grass over
wildflowers.

◉ **Use climbing plants:** crawling up the side of your house, all over your giant
water butt, or up trellises and pergolas, climbing plants can provide shelter and
food for birds and insects. Some top climbers: ivy (perfect for nesting blackbirds),
honeysuckle, bramble (if you can keep it under control).

4. Make artificial habitats

Depending on where you live, man-made habitats may help to encourage useful garden wildlife. Our contemporary tendency to tidiness in the countryside and in parks and gardens has reduced the living space for many creatures, who like hollowed-out dead trees and rotting wood.

Artificial-habitat tips:

- **Put up some nest boxes:** it is possible to provide alternative shelter for a huge range of birds, from blue tits to barn owls. Nesting-box design is key, for the size of the entrance hole determines which types of bird can fit in. Nesting boxes can be bought at garden centres or through the RSPB; or their designs can be copied and knocked up at home: most nest boxes are easy to make. Bats, another useful species increasingly denied habitat, can also be persuaded to take up residence in nest boxes, as can hedgehogs.
- **Make insect habitats:** an untidy wildlife garden will most likely provide excellent habitats for insects, but there are a few steps you can take to be sure of attracting useful species. Solitary bees, which are excellent pollinators, like to live in tunnels: you can buy pretty 'bee hotels' for this purpose or simply drill holes from 2–10mm in diameter in a thick piece of wood and fix it to a sheltered wall. Lacewing larvae and adults are prodigious consumers of aphids and can be encouraged to overwinter in rolled-up corrugated cardboard stuffed into a plastic bottle and hung from a tree. Compost heaps (see pp. 48–51) harbour a vast amount of insect life too.
- **Build a stone wall:** rough walls with lots of nooks and crannies are ideal for spiders, toads, beetles and bumblebees.
- **Pile up some logs:** logpiles provide a home for insects, hence food for birds and for small mammals who might also live there.

5. Provide food

From a bird table to plants chosen for their value to wild creatures, the 21st-Century Smallholder's outside space or garden can easily entice a variety of species.

Food-providing tips:

- **Plant things that will provide food all year round:** the garden can provide a source of food when it might be scarce elsewhere. By choosing early- and late-flowering plants you can help insects like bumblebees that have just emerged for the spring or those which are just about to retire for the winter. Leaving flowerheads to form seed will provide food for birds.
- **Put up a bird table:** which could be the main source of food for some birds in a hard winter. Take care to site it away from any cover behind which cats could lurk.

TOP TEN CREATURES TO ATTRACT TO THE EDIBLE GARDEN

	WHAT THEY DO	HOW TO ENCOURAGE THEM
Frogs and newts	Eat small slugs and young snails	Build a pond.
Hoverflies	Larvae eat aphids	Plant daisies or let umbelliferous plants flower (fennels, parsley, carrots).
Lacewings	Adults and larvae eat aphids	Make a lacewing hotel.
Ladybirds	Eat aphids	Difficult – but they like crevices to hibernate in.
Bumblebees	Crucial pollinators	Provide shaded cover for hibernation and sunny cover for nest sites.
Solitary bees	Pollinators; and their presence indicates a healthy ecosystem	Make a bee hotel.
Wasps	Eat caterpillars and grubs	Provide a nest site – an air-brick in the side of the house is ideal. Encouraging wasps may not suit everyone.
Starlings	Eat leatherjackets, which damage plant roots	Provide nest boxes.
Wrens and robins	Control caterpillars like gooseberry sawfly	Provide nest boxes.
Song thrushes	Eat snails	Difficult to attract: provide lots of 'edge' habitat.

THE 21st-
CENTURY
SMALLHOLDER'S
YEAR PLANNER

January

It's the depth of winter and there's not a lot to do if you don't have much land. Winter vegetables are still cropping well but it's too cold to put much in the ground.

GROWING YOUR OWN FOOD

SOWING, PLANTING AND HARVESTING	
Sow	Under cover: lettuce, salads
Plant	Garlic, rhubarb sets
Harvest	Artichoke (Jerusalem), sprouting broccoli, Brussels sprouts, cabbage (winter), cauliflower (winter), celeriac, chard, chicory, endive, kale, leeks, indoor lettuce, parsnip, rhubarb, spinach

OTHER FOOD-GROWING TASKS
- Force established rhubarb crowns
- Order seeds
- Prune autumn raspberry canes

RAISING YOUR OWN FOOD
- Make sure pigs and chickens are warm and well-fed

STORAGE AND PRESERVING
- Enjoy your stored produce

BUILDING BIODIVERSITY
- Keep feeding wild birds

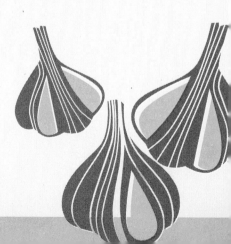

February

The produce year slowly starts to wake up in February. This is the time to begin giving attention to some of the main crops: acquiring and chitting seed potatoes is a priority, and onions and garlic can go in.

GROWING YOUR OWN FOOD

SOWING, PLANTING AND HARVESTING

Sow	Under cover: Brussels sprouts, cabbages, kale, lettuce, salads Outside: broad beans, onions, parsnip, peas, radish, spinach
Plant	Cabbage (spring), garlic, onion sets, rhubarb sets
Harvest	Artichoke (Jerusalem), sprouting broccoli, Brussels sprouts, cabbage (winter), cauliflower (winter), celeriac, chard, chicory, endive, kale, leeks, indoor lettuce, parsnip, rhubarb, spinach

OTHER FOOD-GROWING TASKS

- Put seed potatoes out to sprout (chit)
- Start to prepare ground for sowing; add organic matter to vegetable beds
- Dig up over-wintering brassicas when they are finished

RAISING YOUR OWN FOOD

- Make sure pigs and chickens are warm and well-fed

STORAGE AND PRESERVING

- Enjoy your stored produce
- Perhaps a time to consider preserves made from forced rhubarb

BUILDING BIODIVERSITY

- Keep feeding wild birds

March

If you haven't already pruned your fruit trees and bushes, this is the last chance to do it before growth really starts to kick in. It's time to have a first look at the bees, do a lot more sowing and maybe consider acquiring some pigs if you have the space and the inclination.

GROWING YOUR OWN FOOD

SOWING, PLANTING AND HARVESTING	
Sow	Under cover: beetroot, Brussels sprouts, cabbages, celeriac, celery, kale, leeks, lettuce, salads Indoors, or heated greenhouse: aubergines, peppers, tomatoes Outside: beet (leaf), broad beans, cabbages, carrots (early), onions, parsnip, peas, radish, spinach, turnips
Plant	Artichokes (Jerusalem), asparagus crowns, garlic, lettuce, onion sets, potatoes (maincrop and early), rhubarb sets
Harvest	Artichokes (Jerusalem), sprouting broccoli, Brussels sprouts, cabbage (winter), cauliflower (winter), celeriac, chard, chicory, endive, kale, leeks, indoor lettuce, parsnip, rhubarb, sorrel, spinach

OTHER FOOD-GROWING TASKS

- Last opportunity to prune apples, pears and soft fruit
- Cover land that will not be used until summer by sowing fast-growing green manures
- Cut back shrubby herbs like lavender and thyme

RAISING YOUR OWN FOOD

- Bees: check the hive for food stores by 'hefting' or brief inspection and feed if necessary
- Pigs: a good time to buy weaners for autumn bacon

STORAGE AND PRESERVING

- Enjoy your stored produce

BUILDING BIODIVERSITY

- Keep feeding wild birds

April

The business of food-growing really gets into gear in April. There's a lot to sow under cover and outside, growing seedlings to harden off and pot up and emerging weeds to deal with. The bees will need a little more attention, and now is the time to get started with chickens if you don't already have some.

GROWING YOUR OWN FOOD

SOWING, PLANTING AND HARVESTING

Sow	Under cover: beans (dwarf and runner), celeriac, celery, courgettes, cucumber, tomatoes Outside: artichokes (globe), beetroot, broad beans, broccoli (sprouting and calabrese), Brussels sprouts, cabbages, carrots, chard, chicory, endive, kale, kohlrabi, leeks, lettuce, parsnip, peas, radish, salad rocket, spinach, spring onions, turnips
Plant	Artichoke (globe) offsets, asparagus crowns, Brussels sprouts, cabbage (spring), lettuce, onion sets, potatoes (maincrop)
Harvest	Asparagus (end April), sprouting broccoli, cabbage (spring), cauliflower (spring), celeriac, chard, chicory, endive, leeks, indoor lettuce, radishes, rhubarb, rocket, sorrel, spinach, spring onions

OTHER FOOD-GROWING TASKS

- Feed plants in containers with liquid feed or worm compost
- Weeding
- Earth up early potatoes
- Harden off seedlings started under cover
- Support peas
- Pot on seedlings raised under cover such as aubergines, cucumbers, marrows, peppers, tomatoes
- Enjoy apple blossom . . .

RAISING YOUR OWN FOOD

- Bees: find and mark the queen; put on a queen excluder and honey super if necessary; check for varroa
- Chickens: best time to start chicken-keeping; watch out for broody hens

STORAGE AND PRESERVING

- Enjoy your stored produce

BUILDING BIODIVERSITY

- This is a good time to build a pond or stock it with frogspawn or maybe a bucket of water from a good established pond

May

This is not the best time for the 21st-Century Smallholder to go on holiday. The weeds are growing much faster than your produce and the bees need close attention.

GROWING YOUR OWN FOOD

SOWING, PLANTING AND HARVESTING	
Sow	Under cover: courgettes, cucumber, sweetcorn Outside: Beans (broad, French and runner), beetroot, broccoli (sprouting and calabrese), cabbages, carrots, chard, chicory, endive, fennel, kohlrabi, leeks, lettuce, parsnip, peas, radish, salad rocket, spinach, spring onions, turnips
Plant	cabbage, lettuce, onion sets, potatoes (maincrop and early)
Harvest	Asparagus, cabbage (spring), cauliflower (spring), celeriac, chard, chicory, elderflower, leeks, lettuce, radishes, rhubarb, rocket, sorrel, spinach, spring onions

OTHER FOOD-GROWING TASKS

- Mulch fruit trees and soft fruit
- Harden off seedlings started under cover
- Lots of weeding
- Mulch established vegetable crops
- Pinch out tomatoes
- Earth up potatoes
- Support peas
- Thin out beet, carrots, lettuce, parsnip, radish, spinach, turnip if sown direct
- 'Pot on' seedlings of aubergine, celeriac, celery, courgettes, cucumbers, peppers, tomatoes
- Keep an eye out for pests

RAISING YOUR OWN FOOD

- Pigs: a good time to buy weaners for early autumn pork
- Bees: probably the busiest month in the beekeeping year. Inspect the hive weekly. Add honey supers as required; take an early honey harvest if appropriate (if oilseed rape is nearby, honey must be removed immediately because it crystallizes in the comb). Check for signs of swarming and artificially swarm if necessary. Ideally, have a spare hive available.

STORAGE AND PRESERVING

- Do anything possible to extend the elderflower season: making elderflower champagne or syrup is best

June

For our forebears, who were utterly reliant on their own produce, this was one of the hungriest times of the year, with the winter crops gone and the summer maincrops still not ready. However, today it's a time to start enjoying your produce in a big way, as early fruit and veg crops start to kick in.

GROWING YOUR OWN FOOD

SOWING, PLANTING AND HARVESTING

Sow	Outside: Beans (French and runner), beetroot, broccoli (sprouting and calabrese), cabbages, carrots, chard, chicory, courgettes, cucumber, endive, kohlrabi, lettuce, parsnip, peas, radish, salad rocket, spinach, spring onions, winter squash and pumpkins, swedes, sweetcorn, turnips
Plant	Sprouting broccoli, cabbages, cauliflowers, celeriac, celery, courgettes, fennel, kale, leeks, winter squash and pumpkins, sweetcorn, tomatoes
Harvest	Asparagus, broad beans, beetroot, blackcurrants, broccoli (calabrese), cabbage (early summer), carrots (earlies), cauliflower (early summer), chard, cherries, chicory, elderflower, gooseberries, kohlrabi, lettuce, peas (earlies), potatoes (earlies), radishes, raspberries, redcurrants, rhubarb, sorrel, spinach, spring onions, strawberries

OTHER FOOD-GROWING TASKS

- Prune plums and cherries
- Net fruit bushes, raspberries and maincrop strawberries
- Weed, hoe and mulch
- Pinch out and stake tomatoes
- Thin out beet, carrots, lettuce, parsnip, radish, spinach, turnip if sown direct
- Stay vigilant against garden pests

RAISING YOUR OWN FOOD

- Bees: continue weekly inspections if the colony has not swarmed. Remove honey if oilseed rape is nearby and make sure bees have sufficient food.
- Chickens: check them for parasites as the weather warms up

STORAGE AND PRESERVING

- Dry out and string up onions and garlic for storage
- Freeze broad beans and peas if you have a glut
- Time to start preserving gluts of fruit

July

The first mad flush of spring growth calms down, making weeding a little easier; and the bees need less vigilance. Drying a substantial onion crop now will give you a long-term supply of this culinary staple.

GROWING YOUR OWN FOOD

SOWING, PLANTING AND HARVESTING	
Sow	Outside: beetroot, chard, chicory, courgettes, cucumber, endive, kohlrabi, lettuce, parsnip, radish, salad rocket, spinach, spring onions, winter squash and pumpkins, swedes, turnips
Plant	Broccoli (sprouting and calabrese), Brussels sprouts, cabbages, kale, leeks
Harvest	Apples, artichokes (globe), beans (broad, French and runner), beetroot, blackberries, blackcurrants, blueberries, broccoli (calabrese), cabbage (summer), carrots (maincrop), cauliflower (early summer), celery, chard, cherries, chicory, courgettes, cucumber, elderflower, fennel, garlic, gooseberries, kohlrabi, lettuce, onions, peas (maincrop), potatoes (earlies), radishes, raspberries, redcurrants, rhubarb, sorrel, spinach, spring onions, winter squash and pumpkins, strawberries, turnip

OTHER FOOD-GROWING TASKS
- Pinch out and stake tomatoes
- Water and feed celeriac, celery, courgette, cucumbers, leeks and potatoes and tomatoes in containers
- More weeding, hoeing and mulching

RAISING YOUR OWN FOOD
- Bees: harvest honey (if you want to let them build up their own supplies for the winter)
- Chickens: pay special attention to protein in their diet if they are moulting

STORAGE AND PRESERVING
- Dry harvested onions for storage
- Jam- and wine-making

BUILDING BIODIVERSITY
- Cut spring wildflower meadows

August

The planting tails off rapidly: August is all about enjoying your produce and preserving it when you have a glut (or just fancy some jam).

GROWING YOUR OWN FOOD

SOWING, PLANTING AND HARVESTING	
Sow	Outside: chard, kale, lettuce, spring onions
Plant	Leeks
Harvest	Apples, artichokes (globe), aubergines, beans (broad, French and runner), blackberries, blackcurrants, blueberries, broccoli (calabrese), beetroot, cabbage (summer), carrots (earlies and maincrop), cauliflower (summer), celery, chard, cherries, chicory, courgettes, cucumber, garlic, kohlrabi, lettuce, mulberries, onions, pears, peas (maincrop), peppers, plums, potatoes (maincrop), radishes, raspberries, redcurrants, sorrel, spinach, spring onions, winter squash and pumpkins, strawberries, sweetcorn, tomatoes, turnip

OTHER FOOD-GROWING TASKS
- Keep watering and feeding
- Stake tall brassicas
- Prune apples and pears that are fan-trained or in cordons or espaliers
- 'Stop' cordon tomatoes from further growth to encourage more fruiting
- Thin spinach, turnips
- Cut old leaves of pumpkins and squashes to help ripening

RAISING YOUR OWN FOOD
- Leave the bees alone unless you want to get stung

STORAGE AND PRESERVING
- Even more preserving activity as courgettes and tomatoes start cropping in earnest

BUILDING BIODIVERSITY
- Last chance to put up a lacewing hotel
- Cut hedges when birds have finished nesting

September

The peak of the produce year, with more fresh produce available than at any other time. It's also the traditional time for harvesting honey – a labour-intensive but satisfying task.

GROWING YOUR OWN FOOD

SOWING, PLANTING AND HARVESTING

Sow	Under cover: chicory, radishes, salad rocket Outside: cabbage (spring), endive, kohlrabi
Plant	Garlic, autumn onion sets
Harvest	Apples, artichoke (globe), aubergines, beans (French and runner), beetroot, blackberries, blackcurrants, blueberries, broccoli (calabrese), Brussels sprouts, cabbage (summer), carrots (earlies and maincrop), cauliflower (autumn), celeriac, celery, chard, chicory, fennel, kohlrabi, lettuce, mulberries, onions, pears, peas (maincrop), peppers, plums, potatoes (maincrop), radishes, raspberries, redcurrants, rhubarb, sorrel, spinach, spring onions, winter squash and pumpkins, strawberries, sweetcorn, tomatoes, turnip

OTHER FOOD-GROWING TASKS

- Sow overwintering green manures
- Take nets off fruit so birds can get at overwintering pests

RAISING YOUR OWN FOOD

- Pigs: take porkers to slaughter if bought in late spring
- Bees: harvest honey (if you're going to take the lot and feed them on sugar); start winter feeding

STORAGE AND PRESERVING

- Put maincrop potatoes into a clamp or root cellar for storage
- Furious bottling and preserving activity for fruit and veg

BUILDING BIODIVERSITY

- Sow new wildflower meadows
- Sow hardy annual attractant plants for early flowering
- Net ponds to keep leaves out if necessary

October

Many crops are still in full flow and now is the time to get into serious pickling and preserving mode to get maximum value from your edible-gardening efforts.

GROWING YOUR OWN FOOD

SOWING, PLANTING AND HARVESTING

Sow	Under cover: lettuce (winter), salad rocket Outside: cabbage (spring), endive, kohlrabi
Plant	Autumn-sown broad beans and peas
Harvest	Apples, blackberries, beans (French and runner), beetroot, Brussels sprouts, cabbage (autumn), cardoon, carrots (maincrop), cauliflower (autumn), celeriac, celery, chard, chicory, fennel, kohlrabi, lettuce, onions, parsnip, pears, peas (maincrop), peppers, potatoes (maincrop), quince, radishes, raspberries, sorrel, spinach, spring onions, winter squash and pumpkins, swede, tomatoes, turnip

OTHER FOOD-GROWING TASKS

- Last chance to sow many green manures
- Make a muck heap
- Collect leaves for leafmould
- Prune blackcurrant, blackberry bushes
- Apply greasebands to apple, plum and pear trees to control winter moths

RAISING YOUR OWN FOOD

- Pigs: introduce baconers to your established orchard
- Bees: finish winter feeding; put mouse guards on hive entrances

STORAGE AND PRESERVING

- Drying apples, making cider, jam, chutney, jellies . . .

BUILDING BIODIVERSITY

- Cut summer wildflower meadows

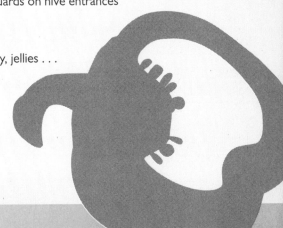

November

It's the end of the road for anything that isn't frost-hardy; but the beginning for crops that are improved by frost such as parsnips and kale.

SOWING, PLANTING AND HARVESTING	
Plant	Autumn-sown broad beans and peas, garlic, rhubarb sets
Harvest	Apples, artichokes (Jerusalem), Brussels sprouts, cabbage (summer), cardoon, carrots (earlies and maincrop), cauliflower (winter), celeriac, chard, chicory, kale, kohlrabi, lettuce, medlar, parsnips, pears, radishes, sorrel, spinach, swede, turnip

OTHER FOOD-GROWING TASKS

- Fork over heavy soils to 'weather' over winter
- Prune red- and whitecurrant bushes

- Pigs: take baconers to slaughter if bought in early spring
- Chickens: make sure their accommodation is well-insulated, water supplies don't freeze and they have a good supply of food

- Put out bird feeders

December

A perfect time to plan the next year's activity, December is also a good time to attend to fruit, planting new bushes and trees and pruning existing ones.

GROWING YOUR OWN FOOD

SOWING, PLANTING AND HARVESTING

Plant	Autumn-sown broad beans and peas, garlic, rhubarb sets
Harvest	Artichokes (Jerusalem), Brussels sprouts, cabbage (summer), cardoon, carrots (earlies and maincrop), cauliflower (winter), celeriac, chard, chicory, kale, kohlrabi, lettuce, parsnips, sorrel, spinach, swede, turnip

OTHER FOOD-GROWING TASKS
- Remove dead fruit from trees
- Best time to plant fruit bushes and trees
- Prune apple and pear trees, gooseberry bushes

RAISING YOUR OWN FOOD
- Make sure the pigs and chickens are warm and well fed

STORAGE AND PRESERVING
- Lift and store parsnips and swedes

BUILDING BIODIVERSITY
- Keep feeding wild birds

Our homes are not sustainable. That is not to suggest that they are all going to fall down any time soon; but they consume more energy and water than the planet can provide and produce more greenhouse emissions and waste than it can cope with. Perhaps surprisingly, only 10 per cent of a building's environmental impact happens in its construction; most of it is during its lifetime, mainly through energy use. The house contributes around one-third of a family's CO_2 emissions (food and transport take the other two-thirds) and domestic energy use accounts for 27 per cent of Britain's overall CO_2 emissions.

MAKING YOUR HOME MORE SELF-RELIANT

Change

Rain

The main reason houses are so hungry for energy is that they are, on the whole, badly insulated, so when the weather gets cold the fossil-fuel demand rises sharply. (At the time of writing, a cold winter has pushed the EU's CO_2 emissions back on an upward trend when they should, ideally, be falling rapidly.) Culturally, thanks to cheap fossil energy and efficient central heating, we've become accustomed to houses that are warm and cosy throughout. Our homes today are on average ten degrees warmer inside than they were in the early 1900s, when costlier and more cumbersome coal fires meant that only the occupied rooms were heated.

But any energy efficiency brought about by the slow spread of better heating systems, insulation or glazing through our housing stock has been cancelled out by our fondness for electricity-guzzling appliances. Between 1990 and 2002, home energy use actually rose by 10 per cent, thanks largely to growing numbers of computers and appliances on standby.

What with global warming, peaking oil supplies and the UK's increasing reliance on vulnerable gas supplies for power and heating, domestic energy use makes me nervous.

Our Western lives also guzzle water like it was going out of fashion (which, thanks to climate change and usage patterns, it may well be). The average UK citizen uses 150 litres of fresh drinking water per day, of which nearly half is used by toilet-flushing, laundry, washing and bathing. With the average toilet flush at around 8 litres, one trip to the loo uses nearly twice as much drinking water as an inhabitant of Saharan Africa might use each day, for all their needs.

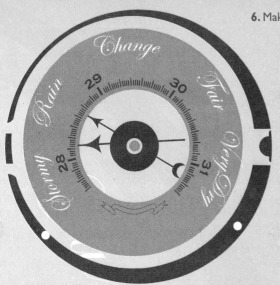

And we could use our waste products more efficiently too. The thought may make you squirm with disgust; or you may simply see it as a retrograde step to a filthy, old-fashioned way of doing things, but wee and poo are valuable commodities. Urine can activate compost and feed plants; and faeces, properly treated by lengthy composting, can, for example, fertilize your fruit bushes with no risk to health.

Anyone reeling at the thought of a composting toilet should simply answer this question: do you want to live next to a sewage farm? Thought not. But, thanks to the way our systems are currently ordered, someone's got to, whether they like it or not. I want to live next to a sewage farm like I want to live next to a landfill site, waste incinerator or power station, which is not at all. But my current lifestyle demands that these places exist.

In *The Earth Care Manual*, author Patrick Whitefield notes, simply and trenchantly, that 'In ecological systems, there is no such place as "away"'. Nature has no cesspits, no middens, no slag heaps. It is instead characterized by re-use and recycling: it is full of 'closed-loop' systems that take care of themselves; human society is not.

This question brings us to the whole point of why a 21st-Century Smallholder should be worrying about energy and water. As with food, it's about taking control, taking responsibility and doing things that are more sustainable. It's not necessarily about achieving self-sufficiency – although in certain circumstances, energy and water autonomy is possible – but about reducing your reliance on unsustainable sources. And it's also about making a contribution: one solar hot-water panel won't make a difference, but a panel on every house will shut down a few power stations.

Our smallholding forebears had no choice but to take responsibility for their own energy, water and waste. In their time, it was a question of survival. In our time, many people will quite legitimately question the sanity of taking such responsibility, say, by installing a costly solar electric system or a composting toilet, when there's already an electricity grid and a sewage network. It might seem like affectation; like a bit of green grandstanding. But most of the people who invest in such systems do so out of a deeply held conviction that they want to be part of the solution, not part of the problem; and that they want others to see what's possible too.

There are people out there generating more power than they use, slashing their heating bills or even becoming completely 'carbon neutral'. And many of them are doing this from normal, boring, existing houses, not from dream 'eco-houses' that only a fortunate few of us will ever get to build or live in.

It's not hard to make moves to a more 'self-reliant' home; many of the actions you can take are quick, cheap and effective. Sure, many of them are also ridiculously expensive and have payback times that stretch into decades. But most of them are satisfying and some are even fun. And, as with any aspect of being a 21st-Century Smallholder, there will be something in this chapter that works for you.

Saving energy

The arguments for saving energy are difficult. We currently live in a world of energy abundance and, on average, just 3 per cent of our total household expenditure goes on heat and power. On average, that's around £600 a year. Such is the affordability of power that by 1994 we used 50 per cent more electricity for lighting and appliances than we did in 1970. If it's about saving money, then we can do it much more quickly and effectively by buying fewer clothes, holidays, cans of beer or tankfuls of petrol. If money is tight, however, then there are a few energy-saving actions that will save money straight away, albeit at the cost of some comfort – for example, turning down the thermostat and putting on some extra jumpers. But many energy-saving measures involve investment: loft insulation may not be particularly expensive, but it still costs money and the payback is long and gradual. And big, serious energy-saving measures like cladding your house in a layer of insulating material cost big, serious money: an investment you may never recoup.

So until fuel costs go through the roof, you have to care about saving energy – to think it's worth the (fuel-efficient!) candle – before you take steps to do it. I think there are two reasons for caring: the altruistic and the personal. The former is predicated on a belief that there is an energy problem. And there is a vast weight of evidence to suggest that there are two big energy problems. The first is that the supply of fossil fuels, in particular oil, has peaked. Britain is fast losing any autonomy in fossil fuels it had; and our move to gas-fired power stations means that in a few years' time we will be dependent on dwindling supplies piped from unstable regions of the world. Renewables are developing slowly and even if it didn't terrify many of us, a nuclear renaissance might not happen in time. The other big energy problem is of course 'anthropogenic' (human-generated) climate change, seen now by all but a few self-interested nay-sayers in the fossil-fuel industry as the defining crisis of this century. In a world that likes grandiose technical fixes: 'The hydrogen economy!' 'Windfarms everywhere!' 'Nuclear power, yes please!' – the boring, prosaic fact is that energy efficiency could go a long way to solving both the power problem and the carbon dioxide problem.

The altruistic reason for saving energy is therefore all about seeing yourself and your household as part of the solution to these twin energy crises, for it is certain that in the future energy will not only cost more, but we will be forced to use less by the demands for CO_2 reduction. In the short term, therefore, there's little in it for you; but your energy-saving actions are making a contribution to solving a future problem.

The personal reason is all about reducing dependence. Personally, I don't like the idea of being beholden to an energy network that has a deeply uncertain future; and I'm uncomfortable that my home belches more greenhouse gases than it should. For purely selfish reasons, I'd like to lessen my feeling of dependence by making my home use as little energy as possible.

Living a more 'sustainable' life, being less dependent: taking control of energy use is all part of being a 21st-Century Smallholder.

As this chapter shows, there are a lot of ways to make a difference, some cheap and easy, some costly and complex. But they're all worth a look; and, in my view, many of them will be standard practice before too long.

Changing behaviour

This is the cheap and easy bit. We keep our houses at 20+°C because, unless we're poor (or worse, old and poor), energy is relatively cheap and we don't notice the cost. The humble central-heating thermostat could, however, make a big difference to our energy consumption. Every degree centigrade you turn it down reduces your bill by around 10 per cent. As the Energy Saving Trust (EST) points out, if we all dropped our thermostats by one degree during the heating season, we would save over £650 million worth of energy and 9 million tonnes of CO2 emissions every year. Rather that than a new nuclear power station or windfarm at the end of the garden. Peter Harper of the Centre for Alternative Technology ran an experiment to see how his family reacted to thermostat changes; in a week, people had become accustomed to 16°C, setting his heating bill up for a 50 per cent reduction straight away. Any lower than 16°C, though, as Peter pointed out, and you're into thermal-underwear territory, which is not everyone's thing; but for those really committed to this quick, cheap and highly effective way of saving energy, there are a lot of cheap and cosy fleeces on the market these days.

The thermostat is the biggie, but there are other cheap and easy energy-saving measures:

- Turn off the lights – unless you need them.
- Drop the hot water cylinder thermostat to 60°.
- Switch off appliances on sleep or standby – a single TV that spends its downtime on standby consumes 53kWh per year of electricity.

Buying efficient stuff

And this is where you have to spend in order to save. Some energy-efficient appliances are comparable in cost to the energy-guzzlers: fridges, for example. Others, like compact fluorescent lightbulbs, cost more but last up to twelve times longer and – suggests the Energy Saving Trust – can save up to £7 per bulb per year on your electricity. A list of products carrying the EST's 'Recommended' stamp can be found at www.est.org.uk.

Improving your house

The next step to take is to help the place in which you live use energy more efficiently. This is difficult for those in rented accommodation, who may lack both the permission and (quite rightly) the motivation to spend money making their flat or house more energy efficient. But for those who are willing and able to tamper freely with their house, here, in ascending order of cost, are the 'basic' steps (i.e. those that don't need changes to its structure).

- **Draught-strip the place.** The older your house, the leakier it's likely to be, with heat escaping between floorboards and around doors and windows. Plugging these gaps is a cheap and effective (if a little labour-intensive) way of helping the house to retain heat. From plugging floorboard gaps with a glue/wood dust mix to using sophisticated draught strips on internal and external doors, and on windows, draught-stripping is an essential part of an energy-efficient refurbishment. Average cost less than £200.
- **Get a high-performance boiler.** If your gas boiler needs replacing, then a modern gas-condensing boiler should replace it. These make use of the heat created when water vapour in the flue gases condenses. With an operating efficiency of 85–95 per cent (as against 65 per cent for standard systems), such boilers can cut bills by up to 40 per cent and pay back in a single year. Average cost £400–800.
- **Fit effective loft insulation.** About 20 per cent of heat escapes through the roof. According to the Government's English House Condition survey 2001, 95 per cent of dwellings with lofts have some insulation, so chances are yours has. But whereas serious green builders suggest a minimum depth of 300mm in order to get a worthwhile effect, the Building Regulations (which dictate how houses should be built) stipulate only 100mm of insulation, or 150mm in less energy-efficient buildings. So most lofts are unlikely to have all the insulation they need. The cheapest way to achieve this with an environmentally friendly, renewable material is to use Warmcel, which is made of recycled paper and can be pumped

quickly into your loft by a specialist installer (or installed at great length by hand). Easier to install but much more expensive to buy is sheep's-wool-based Thermafleece. Average cost £150–200.

Have your cavity walls insulated. With up to 50 per cent of heat escaping through the walls, having them insulated is well worth doing. This is much more of an issue for detached houses than it is for terraced houses and flats, where adjoining dwellings insulate each other (up to a point). Most houses built after the 1930s have a cavity wall that was originally intended to deal with damp: filling this with a waterproof insulating material is an effective energy-saving measure. Today, however, only 36 per cent of cavity walls are insulated. As a rule, the newer your house, the more likely it is to have insulated cavity walls. If you're worried about potential health and environmental issues, then choose mineral wool or polystyrene beads over urea formaldehyde insulation. Average cost £200–400 (with grant, depending on house size).

Fit high-performance glazing. Half of all modern houses are completely double-glazed, meaning there are plenty more to go. If your house needs new windows, then double- or even triple-glazed systems can help to retain the 20 per cent of heat that escapes through the windows. Serious, top-of-the-range gas-filled triple-glazing offers better insulation value than a cavity brick wall. Average cost £500+.

Grants for energy-saving measures in the home are available from the government, energy suppliers and local authorities. The Energy Saving Trust www.est.org.uk has good information on these.

Serious steps

If you've done all this and are still not satisfied that your house is as energy-efficient as it could be, then it's possible to go a great deal further, albeit at more significant cost and effort. It will always be difficult for a 'standard' house (whether new or old) to achieve the efficiency of a purpose-built 'eco-house'. But it is possible to get pretty close, as long as you are prepared to make some serious investment and possibly some structural changes. Again in order of ascending cost, here are the options.

- **Build a conservatory.** Not one of those rather fraught, fiddly designs that goes jutting out into the garden, but a simple 'lean-to' greenhouse style, with an emphasis on width across the house. This provides a 'passive solar' gain and has many advantages, as long as it is separated from the heated house. By creating a pre-heated buffer between part of the house and the outside world, it acts as a layer of insulation. It also warms fresh air entering the house and conducts heat into the place. The house repays the compliment by warming the conservatory in the evening. All of which is also a reminder that conservatories are nice places to be and very good for growing and propagating fruit and vegetables. A south-facing wall is ideal. Average cost £10,000.
- **Fit solar hot-water panels.** This can be a cheap option, if you choose the DIY approach of, say, building a glass-fronted frame around an old black-painted radiator. It's certainly satisfying to know that you get hot water when the sun shines (and even a bit when it doesn't – solar systems can provide 50–70 per cent of your hot water through the year). But solar hot water (whilst nowhere near as expensive as solar electric – see p. 172) is not cheap and has a payback time likely to run to more than ten years. You won't, as for solar electric, need a south-facing roof: panels on west- and east-facing sides will do. But you will need some plumbing and possibly a new boiler. Solar hot-water systems mostly work by pre-heating water in the tank so that the existing fuel source has less work to do. Average cost £1,000–2,000, including grants but excluding extra plumbing work.
- **Fit exterior or interior insulation.** If you don't have cavity walls, then the only way to get better thermal efficiency out of them (apart from the extreme but often appealing option of demolition and reconstruction) is to add insulation, either to the inside or outside of the building. Each approach has its advantages and disadvantages. Insulating the outside of the building avoids 'cold bridging', when outside temperatures are transferred to inside walls. And it doesn't affect the size of the rooms. But it won't be ideal in a conservation area, where cladding a nice brick-built house in, say, 200mm of rendered insulation is unlikely to find favour with the planning authorities. Adding insulation on the inside means slightly smaller rooms and potential 'cold-bridge' problems, but is the only wall-insulation

option for those of us fortunate enough to live in old listed buildings. Cost range £1,000–£15,000.

Ultimately, the measures you take depend on your budget and beliefs. As specialist architect Gil Schalom says, doing something is always better than doing nothing; any of these measures will have an effect on your home's energy performance. Gil and his partner, green activist Penney Poyzer, have, however, taken energy-efficiency measures to extremes in their own home, which they claim is the most comprehensive eco-friendly 'retrofit' in Britain of an existing house. Their project is based on the premise that there will never be enough 'eco-newbuilds' to address the problem of Britain's energy-inefficient housing stock: they wanted to demonstrate what could be done with their Victorian end-terrace house, described by Gil as 'the worst example of a thermal slum'.

See p. 194 for a case study of this house, which also incorporates many other 'green' upgrades (e.g. heating, water harvesting) covered in this chapter.

And the case study on p. 196 illustrates what sort of energy-saving measures are possible when you build from scratch.

Energy saving at a glance

	COST/ HASSLE	PAYBACK TIME	'GREEN' VALUE	THINGS YOU NEED TO KNOW
Behaviour changes	ɯ	ɯ	ɯ ɯ ɯ ɯ ɯ	Anyone can do these and payback is quick.
Buying efficient stuff	ɯ ɯ	ɯ ɯ	ɯ ɯ ɯ ɯ	Worth doing if you are replacing or buying new appliances. Low-energy lightbulbs can have a big impact on energy use. Not worth investing in renewable energy like solar PV until you've done this.
Draught stripping	ɯ ɯ ɯ	ɯ ɯ ɯ	ɯ ɯ ɯ ɯ	Can be hard work in older houses but essential if you are aiming for maximum energy efficiency.
Better boiler	ɯ ɯ ɯ ɯ	ɯ ɯ ɯ ɯ	ɯ ɯ ɯ	Worth doing if you are replacing or buying new.
Loft insulation	ɯ ɯ	ɯ ɯ ɯ ɯ	ɯ ɯ ɯ ɯ	Essential to achieve decent energy efficiency in the home. Needs to be at least 300mm thick to be worthwhile.
Cavity wall insulation	ɯ ɯ	ɯ ɯ ɯ ɯ	ɯ ɯ ɯ ɯ	If you've got cavities, fill 'em. 50% of the heat goes out of the walls.
High-spec glazing	ɯ ɯ ɯ ɯ	ɯ ɯ ɯ ɯ	ɯ ɯ ɯ ɯ	Costly but worthwhile if you are building new or replacing and looking for absolute maximum energy savings.
Conservatory	ɯ ɯ ɯ ɯ ɯ	ɯ ɯ ɯ ɯ	ɯ ɯ ɯ ɯ ɯ	Again, costly but brings many extra practical benefits: propagating fruit and veg, socializing … South-facing is best.
Solar hot water	ɯ ɯ ɯ ɯ	ɯ ɯ ɯ	ɯ ɯ ɯ ɯ ɯ	Needs a few square metres of roof space, preferably south (or SW/SE)-facing. Doesn't work with combination or mains pressure boilers.
External or internal insulation	ɯ ɯ ɯ ɯ ɯ	ɯ ɯ ɯ ɯ	ɯ ɯ ɯ ɯ	A big, expensive step with a long payback time. May have planning implications on conservation areas or on listed buildings. However, essential for high levels of energy efficiency in older buildings.

Cost/hassle: ɯ = free and easy or as near as dammit; ɯ ɯ ɯ ɯ ɯ = possible five-figure sum and professional help needed

Payback time: ɯ = less than 1 year; ɯ ɯ ɯ ɯ ɯ = more than 10 years

'Green' value – subjective score rating overall environmental benefit: ɯ = none; ɯ ɯ ɯ ɯ ɯ = maximum

Generating energy

There is something innately appealing about the idea of being 'off-grid', totally self-sufficient in heat and power. Apart from not getting any bills, there's the sense of security and independence in knowing that power cuts won't affect you. And, if your energy and power generation is from a renewable source, there's the satisfaction of knowing that it's having the lightest possible impact on the environment.

But is such 'unplugging' possible? Or affordable? Or even desirable? The picture is more complex than it seems. Wind and solar power, for example, do not provide 'on-demand' electricity; they only generate when the conditions are right. Switch on the kettle on a cloudy, windless day and your wind turbine and solar panels will not make you a cup of tea. Such systems need storage; storage means batteries; and batteries – particularly of the size that might keep domestic appliances ticking over – bring environmental problems of their own, being made of hazardous, toxic materials. To get over the storage problems, you could install a diesel generator, but that's hardly an eco-friendly option. Going 'off-grid', therefore, has environmental issues of its own; and the relatively small amounts of electricity that often result mean that it is best suited to the 'hardcore greenie' who is prepared to face a life with a bare minimum of electrical appliances: low-energy lighting, or a laptop or two. If you want to use 'green' power, then buying renewable energy from the grid via someone like Ecotricity is by far the simplest way.

So should the 21st-Century Smallholder give up on the idea of generating power at home? Not necessarily. But there's little environmental or economic point in doing so unless you are at the same time taking serious steps to make your home as energy-efficient as possible. Powering electricity-guzzling tungsten filament lightbulbs with a photovoltaic (PV) solar panel would, for example, just be plain silly. At present, there isn't really an economic case for generating your own power. By putting solar PV panels on your roof or installing a micro-wind or micro-hydro system, at the moment you are substituting cheap electricity from the grid for more expensive electricity from your own systems. Without a grant, for example, you won't get your money back from a solar PV system for a hundred years. However, renewable-energy technologies are developing fast and some – particularly wind – can pay back reasonably quickly. And it seems unlikely that fossil fuel prices will be falling in the future.

There may not yet be an economic case but, depending on your views and your means, there is a philosophical case for domestic power generation. You may see it as a way of 'doing your bit' to create a more sustainable energy future. Indeed there is a school of thought that suggests that 'micro-generation' – small, domestic-scale power generation – is the only route to a sustainable power grid, because even renewables cause problems when implemented on a large scale. Witness, for example, the ecological devastation caused by large-scale hydroelectric projects or the nimbyism generated by major wind-power projects. A power grid of the future could consist of thousands of devices built into the fabric of our homes and communities, rather than vast wind-turbine arrays or mighty, CO_2-belching power stations with their accompanying armies of pylons.

If you want to generate your own heat and power, whether for a sense of independence, out of conscience, or even as a building block of a future power grid, the technologies for doing it are all out there. And whilst many are not cheap, they are rapidly becoming more affordable and more efficient.

Solar electric

The natural world runs on solar power: all living organisms are ultimately dependent on the sun as a source of energy. Human society also, in effect, runs on solar power, because the fossil energy on which 'developed' economies depend is nothing more than captured solar energy from millions of years ago. In *The Whole House Book*, authors Pat Borer and Cindy Harris put the sun's power into perspective by pointing out that the amount of solar energy hitting the Earth in one hour is equivalent to the world's annual demand for fossil fuels.

We hugely under-use the power of the sun to help power our modern British lifestyles. Good building design and the use of a simple technology like solar hot-water generation can go a long way to dealing with our heating and hot-water needs (see p. 167). Solar-generated electricity is a less efficient, more expensive and more high-tech way of capturing and converting the sun's energy. But as long as you're prepared for it not to make financial sense in anything but the very long term, solar PV has a lot going for it. It can, for example, generate as much electricity as a family uses in a year. It looks good – the deep blue of PV panels or tiles combines with their eco-friendliness to create a very benign aura indeed. And it's very low-maintenance and reasonably long-lived. It's 'free' electricity, just sitting on your roof. But it's not for everyone: before getting too excited about the promise of PV, take a look at the 'reality check' list below.

How solar electric works

Solar photovoltaic panels work by using thin layers of semiconducting materials (in most cases silicon) which are adapted to release electrons when exposed to light. The resulting flow of electricity (which increases with the intensity of light) is conducted away by metal contacts as direct current (DC), then carried to an inverter (a small box that will most likely live in your roof space), which converts it to alternating current (AC).

Solar PV systems can either be backed up by battery arrays (for an 'off-grid' system) or, more commonly, they are 'grid-connected': plugged into the mains. This, in effect, uses the electricity grid as a giant battery. It also has the advantage of turning the householder into a potential vendor of electricity, as any surplus can be sold back to the grid. You will need to contact your Distribution Network Operator (DNO) in order to set this up.

What you need for solar electric

- **A south-facing roof.** It's not strictly necessary – within 45° of south facing is OK – but this will give you the best possible PV performance. The roof should also be pitched, at an angle from 15–50°, but ideally at around 35–40°. It should also not be shaded in any way. Solar panels or tiles can be put up in other places: on conservatory roofs or façades, or even as free-standing arrays, but these options (particularly the latter one) may have extra cost and even planning implications.
- **At least 10 square metres of free space.** The ideal south-facing roof or sloping space needs to have at least this area free to make a PV installation viable. To generate as much energy as an average family uses in a year (3,300kWh*) would need around 40 square metres.
- **Preferably not to be living in a listed building or conservation area.** Although there are unlikely to be planning restrictions on most PV installations, permission may be needed in some cases: check with your local authority.
- **Upwards of £5,000 to spare.** A 2kWp** system (which will generate half of an average household's annual electricity requirements) will cost in the region of £12,000–14,000. The DTI's Low Carbon Buildings Programme, scheduled to start in April 2006, will provide grants for solar PV and replaces the UK Photovoltaic Demonstration Programme, which ended in March 2006.

Is it worth it?

In pure economic terms, domestic solar electricity is madness. But I'd wager that most people considering PV are not thinking about making a fast buck. They're probably thinking about the other potential 'yields' from solar electricity. There's the feelgood factor; the aesthetics; and the possibility that such a system may add value to your property. There's also a certain element of 'demonstration', too: conspicuous solar panels show others that renewable energy is happening. And who is to say that the payback time won't reduce radically as fossil energy becomes more expensive in the future?

* kWh – a unit of electrical energy (equal to the work done by one kilowatt acting for one hour)

** kWp – the theoretical maximum output for a given area of PV installation

Wind

Britain is windy. We have 40 per cent of the total wind resource in Europe and this could, according to the British Wind Energy Association, meet our electricity needs eight times over. However, wind energy is a highly emotive subject, splitting even members of the green movement, who tussle over the aesthetics vs. sustainability arguments. Perhaps our thinking about wind is going in the wrong direction. Stick hundreds of turbines in an Area of Outstanding Natural Beauty, and even without the powerful, covert goading of the nuclear lobby, people are going to be upset.

Maybe 'micro-generation' is the way forward for wind? It's certainly becoming more accessible. Until quite recently, even small-scale wind turbines were pretty big, meaning that domestic wind-power generation was really only viable for those in possession of a few acres. Today, however, turbines have been developed that are little bigger and arguably a great deal less ugly than satellite dishes, and prices are heading down to levels that make domestic wind-power generation a more practical proposition.

Like solar PV, wind power is an intermittent source, needing either to be grid-connected or backed up by batteries; and it's certainly not suitable for every household. It's cheaper than solar PV, though, so if you have the ideal conditions, it offers a cost-effective and low-maintenance source of clean energy.

How wind power works

Unlike solar PV, there's no real mystery here. The turbine turns a generator which produces a DC current: this is then switched to AC by an inverter and then stored or fed directly into the grid. The power output varies according to the cube of wind speed, so increases in wind make a big difference. Overall, wind turbines will produce an average output over the year of 30 per cent of their rated capacity.

What you need for wind power

A windy site. Goes without saying, really; but the energy yield of wind turbines is radically affected not only by the amount of wind, but also by its quality: if the wind is made turbulent by buildings or mitigated by trees, then a turbine is unlikely to be viable. So in Britain, this means clear exposure to the south-west, from where our prevailing wind blows, preferably uninterrupted by buildings, hills or trees. The presence of anything higher than your turbine site within 100 metres is likely to make it unviable. For house-mounted turbines, a south-west-facing gable end is ideal. Being high up, in the north or west of England, or preferably Scotland, Wales or the Pennines, is also a distinct advantage.

In practice, all this means that many houses in both urban and rural areas will not be suitable for domestic wind generation. However, there are a good few that will be, and the benefits for such houses are likely to improve, as the technologies are developing fast.

Planning permission. For all but the tiniest battery-charging toy turbines, you are likely to need permission from your local authority. This currently applies to the new generation of 'house-mounted' small turbines as well as the more serious 'stand-alone' machines. There are, however, moves to ensure that small-scale wind generation is readily granted permission, so this hurdle should become easier to clear over time.

Upwards of £1,000 to spare. The smallest turbines, designed to be fitted directly to a house, are now heading down towards the £1,000 mark, installed. For this price, you get a 1kW system. The cost rises with power, with systems in the 1.5kW to 6kW range costing £4,000–8,000 installed. The costs are, of course, higher for stand-alone, off-grid systems that need battery or diesel-generator backup. Grants are available – see below.

Is it worth it?

As long as you have an ideal site for wind generation (and this is crucial to making it viable), then wind generation makes economic as well as environmental sense. In theory, a 1kW turbine could provide 80 per cent of an average family's entire annual electricity needs, paying back in around six years. Systems have a lifespan of between ten and twenty-five years, so the more robust ones could go on to provide free electricity for a good few years.

Micro-hydro

Domestic hydroelectricity? Are you serious? Well, yes, it can be done. 'Micro-hydro' systems (those that generate less than 100kW) are indeed available for the householder. And there's nothing new about this: small-scale hydroelectric schemes were once common in areas such as Wales in the early twentieth century, before the arrival of the National Grid put them out of business. But this particular form of renewable energy generation is highly location-specific. Few of us are fortunate enough to live next to a stream that would be just right for a bit of home hydropower. For those of us that are, however, this is a technology worth investigating. Although the capital costs are high, good micro-hydro systems are long-lived, easy to maintain and provide a more reliable flow of electricity than the wind or sun.

How hydroelectricity works

As with wind power, no great complication here: water turns a turbine, which drives a generator, which produces electricity. Assuming the stream flows all year round, hydro systems produce electricity all the time, albeit at a rate that varies with the flow of water. Micro-hydro schemes are likely to work at about 50 per cent efficiency.

What you need for micro-hydro

A good stream. To get a viable micro-hydro system, you need to be close to the right kind of stream. It should ideally be one that flows all year round and it needs a good enough rate of flow and sufficient 'head' (height) to power a turbine. To generate around 1kW from a micro-hydro turbine, you would, for example, need a flow rate of 15 litres per second and a head of 15 metres. The minimum head requirement is 2.4 metres; but the lower the head, the higher the flow rate needed.

Professional help. You could go down the DIY route, but only if you're an engineer or seriously talented hobbyist. You will need help to assess the site, choose the right type of equipment and build the infrastructure (intake, powerhouse, outflow, cables).

Permission. Micro-hydro schemes are likely to need permission from both the local water company and the Environment Agency (SEPA in Scotland), who will assess them for environmental impact. Building weirs and dams necessitates further permissions.

Around £20,000+. Capital costs for micro-hydro are high, with the 5kW needed to power a house costing around £10,000 in fixed costs and around £2,500 per kW. Grants are available – see below.

Is it worth it?

Bizarrely, yes, in the long term and if you have the right site. If you are grid-connected, then sales back to the grid (combined with savings) could bring payback in under a decade. And if you are in a remote location, then the cost of a grid connection could make the prospect of even such a significant investment in renewable energy attractive.

Combined heat and power (CHP)

CHP differs from wind, solar and hydro in that it doesn't use renewable energy. The systems that are becoming available for home use are powered by natural gas: although CHP systems using biofuels (organic matter of recent origin) are being developed, these are not currently viable for the householder. However, domestic CHP is an interesting energy-saving technology: a unit similar in size and appearance to a conventional gas boiler generates heat and also produces electricity. Whilst fossil-fuel-powered CHP is not a 'sustainable' source of electricity, it does bring about efficiencies, with a claimed reduction in CO_2 emissions of 1.5 tonnes per household per annum.

How CHP works

Domestic CHP units use Stirling engines, in which pistons are powered by the repeated heating and cooling of gas in a cylinder and move through an alternator in order to produce electricity. The heat output of this process is then used to heat water in the same way as a conventional boiler.

What you need for domestic CHP

A reasonably well-insulated house. The heat output of a typical CHP unit means that it works best in a house with a heat loss of around 8kW, which generally means a new five-bed detached house, a 1990s four-bed detached house or a 1970s three-bed semi.

About £3,000. Domestic CHP units cost more than even the fanciest energy-efficient boilers.

Is it worth it?

If the cost of solar electricity is too scary, wind isn't viable and you don't live next to a powerful stream, then a CHP unit is the next best way of generating electricity at home. Its proponents claim savings of £150 per year, including the proceeds of your sales back to the grid.

Biofuels

You won't generate electricity with biofuels, but you could heat your house with them. The term 'biofuels' covers everything from 'energy crops' like corn fermented and turned into ethanol to power cars, to methane; from sewage and landfill, to burning agricultural wastes and wood. On a domestic level, biofuels basically means wood. Even the hardest of hardcore environmentalists is unlikely to have the stomach for a home-based methane digester, producing gas for cooking from a foul-smelling slurry of anaerobically decomposing organic matter. Wood does count as renewable energy; and it is 'carbon-neutral', because it absorbs the same amount of CO_2 whilst growing as it does when burnt. However, burning ancient woodland to heat your house is clearly not ideal, so finding a sustainable source of fuel is important, as is finding the most efficient way of burning it. Fortunately, both fuel supplies and wood-burning technology have come a long way in recent years, so, surprising though it may seem, a good old-fashioned fire can heat your home efficiently and sustainably. The options are either to have a stove for simple space heating, or to have a boiler connected to your hot water and central-heating system.

How biofuels work

They burn and make either you or some water warm. There is a little more to it, in that modern stoves and boilers can achieve very high efficiencies (of over 80 per cent) and with good design and dry fuel can burn with a minimum of pollution. (That crackling, spitting pine log found in the woods and thrown onto a jolly campfire is in fact emitting a worse cocktail of pollutants than any fossil fuel.)

What you need for biofuels

Ideally, not to live in a Smoke Control Area. Smokeless Zones, as they were once called, cover most urban areas in Britain. You can burn fuel in these areas, but it must be of an exempt type and none of the exempt fuels could be described as completely sustainable. However, there is also a list of 'exempted appliances' that can burn wood, so with a little research it is possible to have a sustainable stove in a smokeless zone.

A sustainable source of fuel and somewhere to put it. There's more and more choice for sustainable sources of wood-based fuel. At the high-tech end, wood pellets made of compressed sawmill waste can be used with stoves that feed in the pellets with computerized controls to ensure maximum efficiency. Woodchips from tree surgery and forestry waste can also be used in this high-tech way, although mainly with bigger 'community-sized' stoves. Logs, correctly seasoned for between one and four years to remove moisture, are the most 'natural' option. But it's worth pointing out that for heating, cooking and hot water, even a low-energy household would need around 3 tonnes a year, which takes up a lot of space. And to produce this for your own needs would take a hectare of coppice woodland and a lot of effort. Otherwise, there's the no-cost option: scavenged pallets burn very well indeed.

Compliance with Building Regulations and planning requirements. Heating appliances need to be installed in accordance with Building Regulations (something a professional installer will take care of) and chimneys/flues may need planning permission in listed buildings or areas of outstanding natural beauty.

Upwards of £1,500. Which is about the minimum installed cost for a stand-alone stove for room heating. Pellet- or log-burning systems for water and central heating might cost around £5,000 installed for a typical 15–20kW system. Grants are available. It's worth remembering as well that unless you manage your own coppice woodland or find the wood for free, this is the one renewable energy source that does cost money on an ongoing basis.

Are they worth it?

If you're away from mains gas, it is worth considering wood-burning for both space and water heating. Together with high-spec insulation it can work very efficiently, and for space heating you can't beat the cosiness of a wood-burning stove. If you happen to have a smallish house with a good space for solar water heating (see p. 167), then this, combined with a wood-burning stove with a back boiler and excellent insulation, could be all the heating you need.

Ground-source heat pumps

Not to be confused with geothermal energy, in which heat is extracted from geological heat sources, ground-source heat pumps work in a mysterious way. Using the fact that the ground just a few metres deep stays at a constant 11–12°C all year round, they concentrate this heat into something that can be used for space heating or even to pre-heat domestic hot water. It's not strictly renewable energy, because some power is needed to make this mystery happen, but it uses less power and emits considerably less CO_2 than fossil-fuel heat sources.

How ground-source heat pumps work

There is in fact nothing particularly fancy about this technology: a ground-source heat pump is just a fridge working backwards. Heat taken from the embedded pipes is compressed and concentrated, then pumped around the house via heat exchangers and the chosen heating method. Heat pumps can be used to cool buildings as well, with the ground loop being used to store, rather than generate heat, but this is not efficient for domestic installations. Ground-source heat pumps generate around 4kW of heat energy for every 1kW of power needed to run the heat exchanger and compressor.

What you need for ground-source heat

Space or depth. The key component of a ground-source heat pump is a 'ground loop': a long length of thin pipe that is a closed circuit of water mixed with antifreeze. This either goes into deep boreholes, or into trenches around your property as a straight pipe or 'slinky' coil. Around 80 metres of trench length would be needed for a typical 8kW installation using slinky coil, so if boreholes are impossible, a big garden (that you are prepared to dig up) is essential.

Ideally, underfloor heating. Ground-source heat works with radiators, but these need to be of the right size to deal with lower temperatures of 45–55°C. It works best with underfloor heating, which is effective at lower temperatures. This can be retrofitted to homes but it's not an insignificant task.

- **A very energy-efficient home.** The lower temperatures at which these systems work are not suited to older, 'leaky' buildings. Your home needs to be insulated to high standards before a ground-source heat pump becomes viable.
- **At least £6,000.** Installation is expensive and the distribution system will cost more.

Are they worth it?

Ground-source heat pumps are most viable for houses that don't have mains gas: thanks to the capital costs and the electricity needed to power them, the overall cost is currently slightly higher than gas, although this is likely to change over time. It is possible to run the electrical equipment with battery-supported solar PV for a completely carbon-free system, but this raises the capital costs yet higher. In general, if you have a well-insulated house with a big garden (or the ability to have deep boreholes drilled), and either don't have mains gas or aren't bothered by the higher cost, this is a good alternative, with a long lifespan.

Generating energy at a glance

	Cost/ hassle	Payback time	'Green' value	Things you need to know
Solar electric	🔥🔥🔥🔥🔥	🔥🔥🔥🔥🔥	🔥🔥🔥🔥	Unshaded south-facing roof with 10m² free is essential. May be planning implications if listed or in a conservation area.
Wind	🔥🔥🔥🔥	🔥🔥🔥🔥🔥	🔥🔥🔥🔥🔥	Need planning consent and the perfect windy location.
Micro-hydro	🔥🔥🔥🔥🔥	🔥🔥🔥🔥	🔥🔥🔥🔥	Strictly for those with a handy stream nearby.
Domestic CHP	🔥🔥🔥🔥	🔥🔥🔥	🔥🔥	Need an energy-efficient house. Not renewable energy.
Biofuels	🔥🔥🔥	🔥🔥🔥🔥	🔥🔥🔥	Best not to live in a smokeless zone. Gets very costly for big houses.
Ground-source heat pumps	🔥🔥🔥🔥🔥	🔥🔥🔥🔥🔥	🔥🔥🔥🔥🔥	Big garden or deep boreholes essential. Only works with energy-efficient houses.

Cost/hassle: 🔥 = free and easy or as near as dammit; 🔥🔥🔥🔥🔥 = possible five-figure sum and professional help needed

Payback time: 🔥 = less than 1 year; 🔥🔥🔥🔥🔥 = more than 10 years

'Green' value: Subjective score rating overall environmental benefit: 🔥 = none; 🔥🔥🔥🔥🔥 = maximum

Dealing with water and waste

It is just daft that we use on average around 8 litres of purified drinking water each time we flush away our bodily wastes. This is but one of the many absurdities of the way in which we deal with water and waste. The problem is not that we are all evil, uncaring and profligate. Our attitudes to water and waste – and many of the technologies through which we deal with them – were conceived when water was not considered to be a finite resource and improving sanitation was of primary importance. Today, we know fresh water to be a dwindling resource, abstracted excessively around the world for everything from agriculture to golf courses. And whilst, in the developed world at least, we have solved the sanitation problem, we've done so at the cost of enormous water profligacy. It is ironic that hosepipe bans are the first response to drought in Britain: hosepipes account for a mere 3 per cent of domestic water use, whilst toilet-flushing accounts for over 30 per cent. Being less heavy-handed in the loo does much more to keep water poverty at bay than letting the plants wilt.

However, dealing with water and waste differently is not just about helping to solve a pressing environmental problem: both represent an under-used resource for the 21st-Century Smallholder. Rain, for example, falls mainly down the drain when we could be capturing some of it to water plants (who prefer it to treated drinking water), flush our toilets or even wash our clothes. And although years of social conditioning make it seem unthinkable, our own by-products have their uses too. Urine, when diluted, makes great plant food and can boost fruit and vegetable yields; and composted faeces can provide an effective, free fertilizer. Anyone squeamish about this should know that 54 per cent of the 1.1 million tonnes (dry weight) of sewage sludge we produce each year in Britain is currently used in 'agricultural applications' after treatment. Yum.

There are strong and sensible arguments on both sides of the water and waste debate. For example – as with renewable energy – why go to the trouble of investing in your own system if there's an existing one to plug into? Why invest in an expensive and potentially unnerving composting toilet if you're connected to a perfectly good sewage network? There are ways of being 'green' about water and waste that don't involve going to extremes. But equally, some might feel that the 'extremes' are appropriate: that, for example, dealing with one's own bodily waste should be a household rather than a municipal duty. Whichever side of the debate you're on, changing your relationship with water and waste is worthwhile.

Saving water

Changing behaviour

As with saving energy (see pp. 163–4), simple and easy actions can make a huge difference to your water use. Locking up the hosepipe won't make much of a difference; using the toilet differently will. Pre-1993 toilets use around 9 litres of water per flush; new ones are required to use no more than 6 litres; however, there are dual-flush models available that can do the job with 2–4 litres (depending on what the job is). So simply not routinely flushing away urine is one way: it's pretty benign stuff (unless you've been eating asparagus, in which case it gets a bit whiffy). If this isn't acceptable, putting a device in the cistern to displace water can save up to 3 litres per flush in an older-style toilet. You could try a brick or a plastic bottle full of water, but I couldn't work out how to do this without almost dismantling the toilet. The 'Hippo' is easier: basically a bag made of stout but flexible plastic, it forms a reservoir that confines and saves flush water.

Then there's a long and fairly familiar litany of behavioural changes, all of which will save more than giving up the hosepipe: sorting out any water leaks or dripping taps; taking showers instead of baths; using the dishwasher and washing machine less frequently. As an incentive to these, it's worth getting a water meter fitted, because then these behavioural changes will salve your wallet as well as your conscience. The makers of the Hippo, for example, claim a saving of £20 per year if their devices are used in a metered household.

Gardening differently can also make a difference to water use, although if all your garden watering is from harvested rainwater (see p. 186–8), then it's less of an issue. Some tips for a water-efficient garden:

- **Don't water too often:** so roots will search deeper for water, strengthening the plant.
- **Let the grass grow:** it won't dry out so readily.
- **Make good soil:** soil rich in organic matter retains moisture better (see also p. 57).
- **Use mulches:** which reduce evaporation (see also p. 57).
- **Plant in beds rather than containers:** pots or tubs always need more water.
- **Consider perennial plants:** which often make better use of available moisture.
- **Use targeted watering systems:** like seep hoses or 'leaky pipes'.

More serious steps

If you want to get really serious about saving water, then harvesting rainwater and recycling greywater (see pp. 188–9) can make a big difference. Investing in more water-efficient appliances is also worth considering, particularly as and when existing ones need replacing.

Washing machines and dishwashers account for over 20 per cent of domestic water use. Modern dishwashers now use around 16 litres per cycle, compared with 25 for older machines: as long as they are used only when fully loaded, this makes them more water-efficient than washing up by hand. The latest washing machines now use 50 litres per load; rather older appliances', 100 litres. And all such appliances now carry energy labelling (from 'A' for best to 'G' for worst) that details water as well as electricity use. Even with a metered supply, converting to modern appliances won't necessarily pay back financially over the average eight-year life of an appliance, but this may change over time.

Targeting the toilet and the taps can also make a big difference. Replacing a perfectly good bog is a needless expense, however, so using something like a Hippo (see p. 185) is the best way if you don't need a new one. It is also possible to fit an 'Ecoflush' device to some toilets to control the amount of water used. If, however, you are refurbishing or building a house, a low-flush toilet such as the Ifö Cera costs a little more to buy, but with half the water use of a standard loo it will pay back a metered household over time. More extreme sanitation solutions are dealt with in 'Sewage alternatives' (pp. 190–3). Spray taps and low-flow shower heads can also be fitted to reduce water use.

Harvesting water

Capturing rainwater for use in the garden or the home is an option available to anyone with legitimate access to a drainpipe. Although rainwater may not be recommended for drinking, it is said to be preferable to tap water for garden irrigation because plants don't like the chlorine residues in drinking water. And, as for toilet flushing, it does seem daft to shower plants with purified water when, first, they would prefer something else and, second, it's an increasingly pressured resource. You can go a lot further than just a simple water butt, though: it is possible to use harvested rainwater for washing clothes and flushing toilets and even, at the extreme end, for drinking and washing.

Rainwater for the garden

This is cheap, simple and will benefit any garden. Water butts storing over 200 litres can be bought for a little over £20: all they need for installation is some space near a drainpipe and a diverter which is easily fitted to the pipe. Such tanks will be quickly emptied during dry periods, so if the garden demands a lot of watering (for example if you are raising lots of seedlings) it's always ideal to buy the biggest possible butt. Recycled tanks up to 1,500 litres and beyond are available and, although large, such monsters can either be buried or disguised with climbing plants.

Rainwater for the house

Even if you live in a relatively dry part of Britain, a lot of water falls on your roof. Over 45,000 litres a year run off the roof of my terraced house in London, of which I could capture around 30,000 litres. If my family went for drastic water-efficiency measures to get our consumption down to, say, 25 per cent of the national average, then we could, in theory, supply all our needs from rainwater. But we'd need somewhere for around 4,000 litres worth of storage tanks and some sophisticated filtering equipment. Relying completely on rainwater is an expensive and potentially hazardous business, and highly dependent on where you live and how suitable your roof is. For example, parts of the east and south-east of England receive only 500mm per year, whilst the Lake District and Snowdonia can get soaked by over 2,400mm.

Still, as purified drinking water is an increasingly precious resource, it doesn't seem to make sense that we use it for so many applications where rainwater would do the trick. Most commercially available rainwater-harvesting systems are focused on using the water where it needs minimal filtering – i.e. washing clothes, flushing toilets and watering the garden. Together, these take up over 50 per cent of domestic water use. To use rainwater for drinking and washing, however, adds an extra layer of complexity and expense, as filters need to be installed and maintained throughout the system. And to rely exclusively on rainwater you will additionally need to be absolutely sure of your house's ability to capture enough: for many houses, in many parts of the country, it won't be possible.

If you want to be more autonomous in water, or simply feel it is right to invest in using it more efficiently, then rainwater harvesting for the house is possible, albeit at some cost.

What you need for domestic rainwater harvesting

A supply of water: to calculate how much water falls on your roof, you need to know the local annual rainfall, and the area of the roof. These figures are then multiplied with a 'runoff co-efficient' (which relates to how efficient your roof is at delivering water) and a 'filter efficiency' score, relating to losses in the water filter. So for my house, with a reasonably efficient and generously sized pitched roof, the calculation would be:

London rainfall (mm)		Roof area in square metres		Runoff		Filter efficiency	TOTAL
630	×	72	×	0.75	×	0.9	30,918 litres

To calculate how big a tank you might need, assess your daily requirement in litres and multiply this by a guess at what the longest period without rain is likely to be.

So a rough guess for a family of four each using water at the current average level (150 litres per person per day) and wanting to use rainwater for half their needs might be:

Daily usage (litres)		Days without rain		Half of needs	TOTAL
600	×	21	×	0.5	6,300 litres

Which is a monstrous tank; and which illustrates that the current average levels of water use (600 litres a day means 219,000 litres a year) need to be cut radically with water-saving measures before rainwater harvesting becomes viable.

Space for a tank: the rainwater tank will need either to be buried (under the drive or the garden, for example), or installed in a cellar.

Upwards of £2,500: the system will need to be professionally installed and work will be needed to plumb it into your existing water system so that the right water flows to the right appliances (mains to the taps, rain to the toilets and washing machine).

Greywater recycling

'Greywater' is the rather murky term for the murky stuff that swills out of sinks, bathtubs and showers and off down the drain. Recycling greywater can save up to 18,000 litres per person per year, or a third of daily household use, mainly by using it to flush toilets. So why don't we all do it? Because recycling greywater is a tricky business. It needs to be stored somewhere in order to be used; and because it tends to be warm and full of bugs, greywater deteriorates quickly in quality when stored. So to prevent this happening it needs to be filtered and treated; and also pumped high into the house so it can be gravity-fed to the toilets. This means building and plumbing in a sealed system.

Easier ways of recycling greywater are simply to chuck a bowl of washing-up or bath water around plants. However, even this can be problematic because the salts in soap can damage the soil.

On the whole, domestic greywater recycling on anything other than an 'occasional bucketful on the garden' basis is expensive and generally considered impractical for even the greenest of households to consider. If you live in a dry area, pay for mains drainage, and do a lot of gardening, then it may well be worth considering using a reedbed as a way of dealing with greywater: it could reduce your sewage costs and also produce a resource. As Patrick Whitefield points out in the *Earth Care Manual*, reeds are a useful source of mulching material.

Sewage alternatives

In a foreword to Peter Harper and Louise Halestrap's *Lifting the Lid: an ecological approach to toilet systems*, environmental campaigner George Monbiot comments that: 'Every time we pull the chain, the future of the world is sucked a little further down the drain.' He's referring to the fact that conventional flush toilets are designed to use excessive amounts of fresh drinking water to do their job. But the 'bog standard' toilet goes on to commit an even worse crime: it then contaminates this precious stuff with human waste (that itself could otherwise be turned into a valuable natural resource), mixing all into a vile sludge needing industrial treatment at large, unpleasant facilities.

So as part of creating a more environmentally friendly, self-reliant house, should we automatically look at radical ways of dealing with our waste? Not necessarily. As Harper and Halestrap point out, the flush toilet does a lot of things well: it is hygienic, efficient, reliable and socially acceptable. And for most houses in cities, towns and villages, it is plugged into an existing sewage network which, although ecologically illogical, works well and has preserved public health for many years.

There are many ways of dealing with human waste differently, from the simple to the extreme. Which – if any – you choose to use depends on several things: where you live, your budget, your sensibilities and your personal philosophy.

Basic steps: cheap and easy sewage alternatives for all

Because flushing uses so much of it, many of the things we can do to make our toilets less destructive have to do with saving water. Using displacement devices in the cistern (see p. 185) can save 3–4 litres per flush. And following the axiom 'If it's brown, flush it down; if it's yellow, let it mellow' can save even more, but this is not to everyone's taste.

But what possible way is there of using waste differently without exposing the household to unpleasantness and risk? According to the authors of *Lifting the Lid*, urine is, with the exception of some rare tropical diseases, non-pathogenic and 'almost certainly the best fertiliser you can obtain and it's free'. This isn't a licence to start peeing willy-nilly all over the vegetable beds, because neat urine will 'burn' the plants and contains high levels of sodium they won't like. Diluted at around 1:20, however, its valuable nitrogen content can be delivered directly to growing plants. Application is easy, particularly for men: who is to know that you had a sly pee in the watering can before topping it up from the water butt?

Fresh urine, in modest quantities, is also famed for 'activating' sluggish compost heaps (see p. 49).

Also cheap and easy, but perhaps offending more sensibilities, is a way of 'composting' urine. The 'straw-bale urinal' could lurk in a discreet, shady corner of a larger garden: nothing more than a straw bale with the cut ends uppermost, it is peed on intermittently then left for six to nine months: a fine compost develops in the interior and the rest can be used as mulch or added to a compost heap.

More serious steps: sewage alternatives that cost money and won't suit everyone

If you are refurbishing a house or simply feel it is right to invest in sewage alternatives, then upgrading your existing toilets is an obvious step. Low-flush models cost little more than standard toilets and use a great deal less water (see p. 185). For a household containing males, a more radical step might be to introduce a waterless urinal. Not everyone's idea of a bathroom adornment, these cost upwards of £250 and deal with the 'odour' problem by using air-freshener pads. There are also air-flushed models available. Depending on the gender mix of a household, waterless urinals can reduce water usage by up to 20 per cent. In the case of these and low-flush toilets, the extra investment can be offset over the longer term by savings in water charges for metered households.

Further up the sliding scale of complexity and potential offences to sensibility is the composting toilet. The mere phrase strikes fear into many; and the 'black hole' of a dry composting toilet can indeed be an unsettling prospect, particularly for those with small, inquisitive children. On the plus side, though, composting toilets do perform a kind of magic, converting faeces into valuable fertilizer that can be used around, say, fruit trees and bushes. (Although the resulting compost is widely considered to be benign and free of pathogens, it is not recommended to apply it directly to plants that are to be eaten.) And, of course, they produce no sewage, helping your household to be 'waste-neutral'. They don't smell if properly installed and vented and are surprisingly pleasant places to be. Composting systems can also be installed with flush toilets (see case study on p. 195), getting rid of the 'black hole' problem.

Composting toilets are not for everyone, though. Retrofitting one to an existing house, for example, is a serious business. (But it can be done, as the case study shows.) Composting toilets need chambers for the magic to take place: either a large, sloping unit for 'continuous' composting or multiple chambers so that one can be closed when full (the composting process takes a year or so) and a second put into use. Whilst smaller composting toilets are available, ideally you need space: a big cellar or basement space is ideal. They also need not to have too much liquid, meaning ideally that the urine has to be separated out (either by peeing somewhere else or installing urine-separating systems). And as they are, in effect, living ecosystems in their own right, they need looking after: someone, for example, has to indulge in the delightfully named practice of 'peak knocking' from time to time in order to keep the metamorphosing pile of ordure happy.

So unless you have a strong ideological commitment to sewage reduction, a large cellar and either upwards of £2,000 to spare or confident DIY and plumbing skills, composting toilets are probably a step too far for most people looking to 'retrofit' an existing house with eco-friendly features. However, if you are building from scratch, doing an extensive refurbishment of a suitable house, or don't have access to mains sewerage, they merit further investigation and are by far the most environmentally benign way of dealing with human waste.

Water at a glance

	Cost/ hassle	Payback time †	'Green' value	Things you need to know
Changing behaviour	💧	💧💧	💧💧💧💧💧	Anyone can do these and payback is quick.
Buying water-efficient appliances	💧💧💧	💧💧	💧💧💧💧	Low-flush toilets make the biggest difference.
Rainwater for the garden	💧💧	💧💧	💧💧💧💧💧	Easy, cheap and gardens love rainwater. Everyone should have a butt.
Rainwater for the house	💧💧💧💧	💧💧💧💧💧	💧💧💧💧	Need somewhere to put a large tank. Including drinking water makes systems more expensive and complex.
Greywater recycling	💧💧💧💧💧	💧💧💧💧💧	💧💧💧	Too much hassle to be viable for most.

Cost/hassle: 💧 = free and easy or as near as dammit; 💧💧💧💧💧 = possible five-figure sum and professional help needed

Payback time: 💧 = less than 1 year; 💧💧💧💧💧 = more than 10 years

'Green' value: Subjective score rating overall environmental benefit: 💧 = none; 💧💧💧💧💧 = maximum

† Household payback times for water saving are largely irrelevant unless you have a water meter.

Waste at a glance

	Cost/hassle	'Green' value	Things you need to know
Changing behaviour	▮	▮▮▮▮▮	Anyone can do these and big water savings are achieved.
Urine as fertilizer	▮	▮▮▮▮▮	Discretion is advised.
Straw-bale urine composting	▮	▮▮▮▮▮	Even more discretion is advised.
Low-flush toilets	▮▮▮	▮▮▮▮▮	Save water where it is wasted most.
Waterless urinals	▮▮▮	▮▮▮▮▮	Use no water but can be culturally problematic.
Composting toilets	▮▮▮▮	▮▮▮▮▮	Stupendously eco-friendly but need an appropriate location. Recommended to contact appropriate public authorities before installing.

Cost/hassle: ▮ = free and easy or as near as dammit; ▮▮▮▮▮ = possible five-figure sum and professional help needed

'Green' value: Subjective score rating overall environmental benefit: ▮ = none; ▮▮▮▮▮ = maximum

Case studies

Nottingham EcoHome: an 'eco-retrofit'

Despite having been 'the worst example of a thermal slum' when they bought it, Gil Schalom and Penney Poyzer's Victorian semi-detached house in Nottingham is now thought to be the best-performing 'eco-retrofit' in Britain. It is highly energy efficient, produces minimal CO_2 emissions and no solid sewage.

As Gil points out, we will never be able to build enough new environmentally friendly houses to correct the energy-inefficiency of Britain's existing housing stock. And even if we could afford to do it, knocking down all the draughty old houses to replace them with new eco-houses would simply bury the nation in rubble: construction waste makes up 70 per cent of all landfill. 'Retrofitting' existing houses with eco-friendly features has the dual advantage of making sustainable living available to any householder and contributing significantly to reducing the country's overall CO_2 emissions.

The philosophy behind Gil and Penney's project was to turn one of the worst-performing houses into one of the best. Their aim was to upgrade the house's thermal performance as much as they could whilst at the same time aiming to be as autonomous as possible in energy, water, sewage treatment and food. To make their project financially viable, their renovation also included accommodation for a lodger.

Saving energy

Every possible energy-saving feature has been incorporated into the house. The roof was rebuilt and given 300mm of Warmcel (recycled paper) insulation. Thick insulation was also added under floorboards for acoustic insulation as well as to keep the heat in. However, the biggest source of heat loss in a house is the walls, which in the case of this (rather tall) house covered an area of 200 square metres and had no cavity to fill with insulation. So the only options were either to clad the house in a 'skin' of insulating material or to add layers of insulation within rooms. Gil and Penney chose a hybrid approach, insulating inside at the front of the house to preserve its appearance, and cladding it in polystyrene and render at the side and rear. This was one of the most expensive pieces of work, costing £12,000. The house also has high-performance double- and triple-glazed windows and is draught-stripped throughout.

Generating heat and energy

As with all such schemes, Gil and Penney's choices for generating heat and energy were dictated partially by the house and its existing systems. The house had expensive electric water and space heating which meant big savings were possible straight away: a single flat-plate solar hot-water panel has been installed on the south-facing roof and has already achieved payback. Despite the superinsulation, the house is too big to heat with just a wood-burning stove and back boiler (the 'greenest' option), so some form of central heating was needed. Keen to minimize CO_2 emissions, Gil and Penney opted for a high-tech, Smoke Control Zone-compliant wood-burning boiler and heat store rather than choosing gas central heating, the obvious and much cheaper option. At £5,000 after grants, this was one of the most expensive items in the retrofit, but it gives them carbon-neutral heating when they need it and the fuel is free if they can scavenge enough discarded pallets. Two 1m-diameter wind turbines bolted to the chimney are being considered as an electricity-generating option for the future, if planning issues can be overcome; if not, there's room on the south-facing roof for photovoltaic panels.

Dealing with water and waste

The EcoHome has a rainwater-harvesting system that feeds the washing machine, toilets and an outside tap for watering the garden. The water is stored in two 1,000-litre tanks in the cellar and pumped directly to the appliances. A small roof means that rainwater supplies only around 30 per cent of the household's needs at the moment and although not currently bringing savings it is expected to do so if, as is widely anticipated, water costs rise in the future. The rainwater-harvesting system cost a total of £2,000 installed.

Water-saving features in the house include water meters at different points in the system for easy monitoring, and low-flush (2–4 litre) toilets throughout.

Although the house is connected to the sewage system, Gil and Penney were keen, for ideological and ecological reasons, to 'deal with their own shit'. So the EcoHome also features a bespoke composting system, which separates the solids from the low-flush loos and deals with them in a composting chamber in the cellar. Although the system cost £2,000 and needs occasional attention, its use of normal WCs overcomes any issues of social acceptability: and it is likely the EcoHome's fruit bushes will in time be particularly well fertilized!

Tree House, Clapham, London: an 'eco-newbuild'

Keen to build an environmentally friendly house, Will Anderson chanced upon that rarest of things, a building plot with planning permission in central London. The slim site is dominated by a tall mature sycamore tree and Will was captivated by the comparison between trees – built to last, using resources and energy efficiently, recycling everything – and how a house should work. So although high-tech, Tree House has been built with natural principles in mind. The guiding principle of the house is that good design can significantly reduce a house's impact on the environment: in Will's view, cheap fossil fuels are ultimately to blame for much of today's badly designed and inefficient housing.

Building an 'eco-house' from scratch has huge advantages over a retrofit. You are still constrained by the size and orientation of the plot, by surrounding buildings and local regulations; but a new build means you can use the very latest and most efficient techniques and technologies. As Will points out, though, to be truly workable these need to be deployed in a way that is acceptable to everyone involved: his partner Ford was consulted throughout the project.

Saving energy

Tree House is built from a timber frame that allows for a huge thickness of insulation in the walls, between the floors and in the roof. The walls are clad on the outside with wood and insulated with Warmcel (recycled-paper insulation). Windows are high-performance glazed units. Whilst it takes a great deal of effort to insulate an older building effectively, a new build can be completely airtight, providing maximum thermal efficiency. Tree House is airtight and uses 'whole house mechanical ventilation': this takes stale air from places like the kitchen and bathroom and mixes it with fresh air in a heat exchanger to provide heat for living rooms and bedrooms.

Generating heat and energy

Starting with a 'super-insulated' house gives you more options for generating heat and power, because there is much less heat loss. So for space heating, Tree House uses a ground-source heat-pump system, viable only for well-insulated houses. Four 25-metre-deep boreholes were drilled into the ground for pipes which will take the 11–12°C underground heat to a compressor, where it will be concentrated and fed into an underfloor heating system. It's expensive to install (typically from £6,000 upwards) but very cheap to run and the fuel source is free. Electricity for Tree House will be provided by a 5kWp solar photovoltaic array on the south-facing roof. Will anticipates that over the course of a year the house will produce more electricity than it consumes, making it self-sufficient in energy (but not autonomous, as it relies on the grid when the solar panels are not generating electricity). Hot water will be provided by a solar hot-water system.

Dealing with water and waste

Whilst Will believes that there is value in every householder doing what they can towards generating energy, his view on water and waste is that the infrastructure needed for elaborate technologies such as complete rainwater-harvesting systems can often outweigh their benefits. So Tree House will address the 'demand' side of water use, with features such as low-flush toilets, spray taps and basic rain harvesting for the garden. For sewage, Will believes that the location of Tree House in a high-density urban area – and the site itself – would make an alternative solution such as a composting toilet inappropriate.

What if you've looked through this book and completely failed to heed its warnings about the perils of going 'all the way' towards a completely self-sufficient smallholding lifestyle? You haven't been put off by the expense, the grinding toil, or the knife-edge economics of it all. Rather than being a 21st-Century Smallholder — picking from a menu of lifestyle changes — you want to jack in the job, head for the hills and be a real, full-time smallholder. The romantic lure of such an idea is difficult to resist: a life free of bosses and bills, and a cornucopia in your backyard. What would it take to do this? How would you start?

Smallholding is a way of life, not a nine-to-five job. So the best starting point is to ensure that you and your family are prepared to accept a very radical lifestyle change from, say, office workers to modern peasants. And many urban dreamers fail to think about the economics. As land rights advocate and smallholder Simon Fairlie says: 'You can't be self-sufficient in wellington boots.' No matter how close to total self-sufficiency you get, you will still need money to buy stuff and pay the bills. This either means lots of capital or some form of part-time work, especially in the 'start-up phase; and then in the longer term, money-making smallholding activities (which are particularly important if you are going to try to live on agricultural land – see p. 203). Still, 60 per cent of farmers today have an additional source of income, illustrating that not many people truly live off the land.

So in the first instance you should ponder the economics and their practicalities: for example, if a vegetable-box scheme will be the cornerstone of your income, then veg-growing skills would be a distinct advantage. If it's going to be small-scale organic dairy products, then there are yet more skills, start-up costs and infrastructure needed. Your chosen money-making route will also partially determine where your smallholding will be: for example, veg-growing wouldn't be ideal on a steep, wooded site.

But despite the need to focus hard on the economics, the most pressing question for most people considering a truly self-sufficient future is: how do I get my smallholding? There are four main ways of going about it.

How to get your smallholding

1. Do it at home

If you are fortunate enough to have some land already, then self-sufficient smallholding can begin at home, depending on how much space you have. In the classic *Complete Book of Self-Sufficiency* (required reading for anyone wanting to go all the way), author John Seymour suggests that one acre of land (quality permitting) could support a diverse holding with chickens, pigs and a cow as well as extensive vegetable-growing. It wouldn't be true 'self-sufficiency', as you would have to buy in food for the animals and buy in your own cereal crops; but otherwise, such an area could provide for much of a family's needs. Move up to 4 acres and you could theoretically provide fodder for the animals and cereal crops for the family too, creating a complete, 'closed-loop' holding with everything grown on site and an occasional surplus for sale. What would the neighbours say? Well, with all that space you could probably design it in such a way that the neighbours wouldn't notice it too much. And as long as there aren't restrictive local by-laws, you could keep livestock too as long as you had the correct permissions and paperwork (see Chapter 2).

2. Buy a smallholding

In the days of the 1970s self-sufficiency movement, which was kick-started by the decade's oil crisis, chucking it all in and buying a smallholding was a viable option for many. A farmhouse with the necessary few acres of land could be had for an affordable sum. Since then, house prices have increased 35-fold and, unless it is in the far north of Scotland, the perfect place for a smallholding is going to cost hundreds of thousands of pounds. Which is fine if you have enough capital tied up in an existing property to make the move with a small or non-existent mortgage. It's important to keep mortgage outgoings to a minimum because, in order to create a viable smallholding operation, you will additionally need to invest in all manner of kit and infrastructure, whether it's polytunnels, food-processing gear, or wind turbines and solar panels. For those fortunate enough to have the money, however, this is the quickest and easiest way into smallholding: 'peasantry for the comfortably-off'.

3. Buy agricultural land and move on to it

For those of us not already in possession of a fortune in land or cash, this is the most financially viable way towards self-sufficiency. Agricultural land is still relatively cheap and it is possible to live on it. However, this approach is fraught with insecurity. On paper, the government supports 'sustainable development' in the countryside, so eco-friendly, low-impact smallholdings would seem to be in favour. But in practice there is, as Simon Fairlie notes, a 'massive, obsessive, neurotic' resistance at government level to dwellings on agricultural land. This has its roots in an attitude neatly summed up by low-impact roundhouse dweller Tony Wrench: 'The planning system was set in legislation in 1948 to preserve a nice view for toffs and landowners.' Some planning authorities seem to have a policy of resisting any proposals for residence on smallholdings. In the face of this, many people find that the only approach likely to work for them is to move in, live in a tent, caravan or temporary dwelling, start work on their smallholding, put in a planning application and try to get the local authority's refusal overturned at appeal.

Most well-planned smallholding projects do eventually get planning permission, but it can be a long, stressful slog and the effort and insecurity are not for everyone. The key things you need to be able to prove in the planning process are:

- **Financial viability:** supported by a business plan that shows even a subsistence holding making a profit by the end of year three.
  - **A need to be there:** because smallholding is a way of life, of course you need to be there; but the planning authorities are not always receptive to this argument.
    - **Ability:** experience or training in your chosen smallholding activity is helpful.
      - **No other appropriate accommodation:** showing that there is nowhere else available to live nearby.
        - **Sustainability:** any smallholding is likely to be able to provide ample proofs of this; local authorities may not give it weight, but appeals inspectors might.

          Getting involved with the local community so that they are inclined to support your planning applications is also a highly recommended way to increase your chances of success. The case study of Guilden Gate on pp. 212–13 provides some insight into how to create a sustainable single-family smallholding on agricultural land.

4. Do it with friends or family

Smallholdings work best with a 'polycultural' mix of activities – for example, arable farming, livestock and woodland management. So if, say, the crops don't do too well one year, the dairy and timber business can keep you going. And, of course, there's a symbiosis between different activities – such as animals providing fertility for the land – that is lost if your smallholding concentrates on just one thing. The problem is that keeping all this going can be a very tall order for a single family. The livestock side of things alone will tie you to the holding all year unless you have some (skilled) outside help. So a 'community' approach is often more practical. Indeed this is how smallholding was done in the past, at a village or extended-family level, with maybe fifteen or so people involved.

Whether you are buying an existing farm or taking the cheaper but riskier approach of occupying agricultural land, starting out as a community of several families or an extended family has many advantages: shared costs, a mix of skills, many hands making light(er) work. However, a close-knit community is not for everyone, so an alternative is to divide the land into a cluster of more loosely affiliated smallholdings: a 'co-housing' or perhaps 'eco-village' approach. This needs a great deal of co-ordination and agreement between everyone involved; but it offers the benefits of shared effort and expertise without the tight integration of community living.

There are several community smallholdings operating in Britain, each with a different set-up and mix of activities: the case study of Tinker's Bubble on pp. 214–15 shows how one of these works.

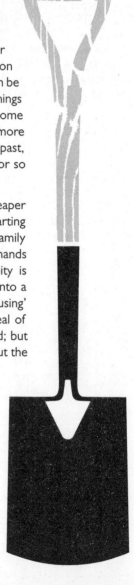

What you will need to make your smallholding work

So you've got your smallholding – what next? Our smallholding ancestors had it easy, at least in one sense: they didn't have to set up from scratch. Land, infrastructure, tools and skills were all passed down from generation to generation. The contemporary smallholder will have to learn many skills and buy or build a lot of stuff. The list which follows gives a basic idea of what you will need to make a smallholding work.

The right kind of land: this is something you should obviously check before buying – it's crucial that the land around your holding can support the mix of activities you plan to do. It is, for example, easier to establish woodland than it is to clear it. The richest and most diverse smallholdings have a balance between grass and trees: this will be determined by the balance of livestock and growing/ forestry activities you are planning. Some other factors to bear in mind in assessing the land include:

Orientation – how much sun/frost/wind might it get?

Slope – is it a problem or an opportunity? Is there any flat land?

Soil – how good is it; what sort is it?

Drainage – are there problems (or opportunities) with water?

Location – where is it in relation to towns, markets, etc?

Planning issues – is it in an area with a special designation (Site of Special Scientific Interest or Area of Outstanding Natural Beauty)? What's the local authority like?

Infrastructure – what have you got? Fences? Buildings? Hard standing?

A plan: planning is crucial to success. Practitioners of permaculture (see p. 29) suggest observing the land over a full growing season before planning in order to find out where the problems and opportunities lie. There's a great deal of sense in this; however, few will have the leisure to be able to do it in full. But in order to build up the holding in a manageable way, experienced smallholders all recommend putting as much time as you possibly can into planning. This means, for example, deciding what's going to go where and when; which activities you will start first; how you will develop your food-growing operation; how the costs will be spread and how much labour is needed.

Water and sanitation: where's the water supply? If you're on a 'bare-land' (agricultural-land) holding, there's unlikely to be any mains, so you will need a viable supply from a spring, stream or borehole. There won't be any mains sewage either, so you'll need a plan for that too (see p. 190 for sewage alternatives or p. 208 'Building an eco-home').

Energy: again, bare-land holdings won't have mains connections, so in these cases generating your own will be the best option (and the most likely to pass the 'sustainability' test). Any woodland on the site could provide fuel for heating; a stream could offer micro-hydro possibilities; a hilltop might suit a windmill and solar is always available as an option, although it's expensive for electricity. (See p. 170 for more on generating energy.)

Equipment: this depends hugely on the type of smallholding. At 'farm level' – over 5 acres – a tractor or multiple horses become necessary; below this, the land could be managed with a small tractor or cultivator or even just a mower, or maybe one horse. Then there are agricultural tools, greenhouses and polytunnels, fruit cages, housing for livestock . . .smallholders need a lot of stuff to get started.

Infrastructure: do you have a farmyard? If not, build one (or the equivalent of one) to avoid the smallholding turning into a sea of mud. Some form of barn is also essential to keep equipment (and possibly animals) out of the weather.

Somewhere to live: if you've bought an existing farmhouse, this won't be a problem: but if it's seriously dilapidated, maybe it's worth knocking it down and starting again. This gives a much better chance of creating a sustainable, energy-efficient dwelling. On a bare-land holding, your accommodation choice in the short term will be dictated by your means and sensibilities: in ascending order of cost and luxury this could be bender, yurt or caravan. In the longer term, your chances of planning acceptance will be enhanced if the permanent dwelling is as eco-friendly and sensitive to the location as possible.

Paperwork and permissions: depending on the type of smallholding, you may need:

Business plan – only required if you are applying for residential planning permission or funding (mortgage or loan).

Land management plan – again, only necessary to support planning applications.

Environmental health approvals – for any form of food processing for sale.

Organic certification – you can't sell produce as 'organic' without formal certification. It is good for marketing but requires much admin and is expensive for the smallholder.

DEFRA animal paperwork – for livestock.

Making a living

Unless you are wealthy enough for it to be a hobby, smallholding has to pay, either by creating an income from produce sold commercially, or by providing the best part of the smallholders' subsistence needs. The insane economics of modern agriculture mean, however, that only certain activities are commercially viable on a smallholding scale. Whilst – as previously mentioned – property prices have risen thirty-five times since the 1970s, wheat prices, for example, are unchanged. Even the large-scale production of grain, lamb or beef is difficult to make profitable today. However, the smallholder does have an advantage, because the lower volumes of produce mean that he or she can process locally and sell direct, via farmers' markets or box schemes. As a result, smallholders can keep the 80–90 per cent of the retail price that is otherwise creamed off by processors, distributors and supermarkets (albeit at the cost of having to process and sell everything themselves).

The table below shows different activities that are carried out commercially on a smallholding scale and also lists 'subsistence' production activities.

COMMERCIAL	SUBSISTENCE
Frequently profitable	Subsistence production on a smallholding goes
Salad bags and polytunnel veg	way beyond home-grown veg and may include
Veg-box schemes and market stalls	many products that have considerable value in
Nursery plants	the outside world:
Free-range eggs	
Pigs	Food (veg, fruit, grain, meat, fat, honey)
Herbs	Water
Apple juice/cider	Sanitation
Chick-rearing	Energy (wood, solar, wind, hydro, horse)
Coppice	Clothing (rarely)
Firewood	Timber and timber products
Mushroom logs	Shelter
Hardwood sawlogs	Entertainment
'Horseyculture' (paddocks for ponies, etc.)	
Harder to make profitable	
Dairy (high processing costs)	
Beef (needs many acres)	
Sheep (also need many acres)	
Honey (pest control can be problematic)	
Field-scale veg	
Softwood sawlogs	
Almost never profitable	
Arable crops	

Building an 'eco-home'

If you are going 'all the way' – as far towards self-sufficiency as possible – then your home will have an impact on your plans. Even though only 3 per cent of household expenditure (around £600 a year) goes on heat and power, such a sum becomes more significant if you are trying to get outgoings down to an absolute minimum. (The similar annual cost of organic accreditation is cited by smallholders as one of their major annual expenses.) It is also highly unlikely that the costs of 'traditional' fossil energy will do anything but rise in the future. And if you are interested in the extremes of self-sufficiency, then chances are you are also interested in consuming minimal amounts of energy for either economic or ideological reasons (or both).

But a home's impact on the environment is not just about energy consumption. A house built from brick, breezeblock and with PVC windows also has high 'embodied' energy, meaning that a great deal of energy has been expended in producing the building materials. And the presence of materials such as PVC or medium-density fibreboard (MDF) means that the house also has 'embodied toxicity': its materials have been responsible either for environmentally unfriendly industrial processes or for residual pollution ('off-gassing' from the urea-formaldehyde bonding, in the case of MDF).

So a home that is miserly in energy consumption and has a minimal impact on the environment is likely to appeal to smallholders for both financial and personal reasons. It is also integral to achieving true 'sustainability', which has perhaps been best defined by the World Wildlife Fund (WWF), responsible for the assessment (quoted in the introduction to this book) that the current British lifestyle needs the resources of three planet Earths to sustain it. The WWF also assessed the roundhouse built by Tony Wrench at the Brithdir Mawr community in Wales. Made largely of locally sourced natural materials, heated by a wood stove, with solar electricity but no fridge, freezer or TV, and with a composting toilet, maximum recycling and some food-growing, the roundhouse scored 'one Earth' – but only just. This is a stark illustration of how much our lives have to change for them to be sustainable; and it also shows how our homes are central to this change.

Building an environmentally friendly house is a huge subject to be covered in a tiny section of a chapter and there are plenty of guides and resources available for those wishing to research the subject in depth (see Further Reading). But here are some pointers to pique your curiosity.

1. Design for minimal energy use

Most 'conventional' housing – from modern houses to ancient country cottages – has not been designed with energy efficiency in mind. Retrofitting can help to put this right (see p. 194), but the 'new builder' can use good design to save up to 90 per cent of the energy a house might otherwise use.

Super-insulate: the ideal is to aim for 400mm of insulation all round, in the walls, the floor and the roof. This can be most easily achieved in timber-framed buildings, where much of the walls' thickness can be made up of insulation, with only thin layers of cladding on the outside and inside.

Orientate the house for 'passive solar gain': with the jargon removed, this simply means making sure that the house makes maximum use of the sun for natural solar heating. At its simplest, this means ensuring most windows face south. If internal walls are of heavy masonry, and floors of tile or stone, these can act as a store that releases heat at night. Adding a conservatory on the south side (see p. 167) can make even more use of the sun, as well as offering other advantages.

2. Choose environmentally friendly materials

This won't necessarily affect the energy efficiency of your house, but it will reduce the 'embodied energy' in its construction, may make for a more pleasant place to live and will also make the house easier to recycle, should this be a consideration. There are always some compromises to be made: for example, maximum energy efficiency is achieved when a building is, in effect, 'airtight', with the airflow managed by heat exchangers (see case study on p. 196). Such high-tech efficiency cannot always be achieved in a house built of entirely 'low-tech' materials: however, such a house may have had a lower environmental impact in its construction; and its owner might put up with the odd draught. Some alternative materials to consider:

Straw bale: modern straw-bale houses do not present the vulnerability that did for the first little pig. Typically, the bales are used in conjunction with a timber frame, then rendered, or clad in timber. As long as the walls are kept dry at top and bottom ('good boots and a good hat'), straw-bale buildings have a long life, are cheap, provide excellent insulation and of course are a renewable, biodegradable resource.

Rammed earth: compressed soil, amazingly, can be turned into bricks or entire walls that are long-lived, environmentally friendly and offer reasonable insulation.

Cob: mud (mixed with a bit of straw) can also make for fine, solid walls that offer good thermal mass and therefore act as heat stores for a 'passive solar' house.

3. Build in features to support a 'low impact' smallholding lifestyle

One of the problems you will encounter as a 21st-Century Smallholder is that the average house or flat doesn't have a lot of the features that are really useful in the business of food-growing, processing and storing. And ultra eco-friendly features like composting toilets are rarely appropriate for retrofits. Bearing in mind the limits of the location, the 'new builder' can design such features in from the start.

Cellar or root store: dark and with a reasonably constant temperature, cellars are ideal for long-term storage of many foodstuffs, but particularly fruit and veg such as apples, potatoes, onions and root crops. If it's too hard to dig one, maybe it's a good excuse to build a small, windowless straw-bale outbuilding.

Pantry: why don't kitchens have pantries any more? Dark but well-ventilated spaces, they are ideal for many of the things that are currently desiccated in the artificial, air-conditioned atmosphere of our fridges.

Conservatory: can also double as a space for raising seedlings if you don't have room for a greenhouse.

Workroom: somewhere to extract and bottle the honey, make the wine (or even the cheese) and store all the kit to do it.

Composting toilet: (see p. 191) if it's appropriate to the site, then it will ultimately help with your fruit-growing and any ambitions towards becoming 'waste neutral'.

Rainwater harvesting: (see p. 186) designing this in from the start will bring savings in the longer term and benefits for the garden too.

Depending on how it is built and which energy features it uses (e.g. solar PV, ground-source heat), an 'eco-home' may be more than 10 per cent more expensive than a conventional house. However, given its potential for keeping financial outgoings (and environmental impact) to a minimum in the longer term, it would seem madness for the smallholder going 'all the way' to build anything else.

Case studies

Guilden Gate organic smallholding

Simon and Jacqueline Saggers established Guilden Gate in 1999 with the aim of 'creating one practical example of what sustainable rural development could look like'. They bought the 2-hectare plot from Simon's family, who have been farming in the village of Bassingbourn for generations. Before starting work on the land, they spent two years planning and researching, learning how to create a farm that is also a diverse, interconnected ecosystem. From a ploughed field they have created a beautiful, richly biodiverse place – a mixture of orchard, woodland, hedges, meadow and vegetable beds – that supports Simon and Jacqueline and their two children and provides a vegetable-box scheme for around twenty-five local customers.

Home and resources

The Saggers took the risky option of building a house on the base of some old battery-chicken houses with only a temporary planning permission. Surrounded as Guilden Gate is by the giant arable fields of eastern England, their application was unusual and it was six years before they received permanent planning permission to live on their holding. Plans for their house had to be modified along the way, but the result is a highly energy-efficient building that is almost invisible amongst the trees and hedges. The cottage at Guilden Gate is timber-framed, super-insulated with Warmcel and clad in local larch weatherboards. For all but three months of the year, heat is provided by passive solar gain and solar water heating; in the coldest months a wood stove supplements these.

The cycle of water use at Guilden Gate is completely closed. 'Water in' for the household and for irrigation is provided by a borehole and buried rainwater tanks. 'Water out' is either filtered and reused, or purified in a reedbed, flowform pond and willow trench. A composting toilet turns solid wastes into fertilizer.

The energy cycle is also closed on the holding with the recent arrival of a 5kW grid-linked wind turbine that will generate more than the family uses in a year. With a capital cost of £15,000, a third of which was paid by a Clear Skies grant, the turbine is expected to pay back in twelve to fourteen years and to be a net contributor to the grid. All the other energy used at Guilden Gate is renewable: wood for winter heating comes from coppice in the holding's woodland; otherwise water and space heating are provided by the sun. Guilden Gate is a net zero CO_2 emissions site.

Economics

Guilden Gate's main commercial activity is their own organic 'veggie'-box scheme which runs from Easter to Christmas and supplies around twenty-five local customers. The box scheme has been built up entirely by word of mouth, without any advertising, and has a lengthy waiting list. The scheme's economics are helped by the fact that the majority of customers, all of whom live locally, collect – and sometimes even pick – the produce themselves. For many customers (and their children), the visit to Guilden Gate is an event in itself and this also helps Simon and Jacqueline to build relations with them. Guilden Gate also produces eggs from a flock of around thirty chickens and honey from five beehives. There are also mushroom logs and, in the future, pigs are planned for the woodland. Despite all this, the smallholding's income form the veggie-box scheme is only around £6,000 per year. However, if the holding's provision of fuel, water, electricity and fruit and veg is counted as income substitution, its income rises by at least another £2,500. In addition, Simon and Jacqueline run guided tours of Guilden Gate and do consultancy and part-time work. The holding's biggest overhead is Soil Association certification (official accreditation is essential if you want to call your produce 'organic'), which costs around £400 annually and is described by Simon as 'like sitting an A-level every year'.

Simon is keen to stress that smallholding is not an easy life, nor is it going to make one financially rich. The planning and project management was long and complex yet essential to creating the successful enterprise that the Saggers now have. The key to being a smallholder, says Simon, is 'to be jack of all trades, willing to fail at all of them but determined to keep trying!' He is passionate about bringing small 'human-scale' agriculture back to the countryside and points out that one of the greatest pleasures is starting to succeed more often than not, as your experience grows. Simon gets the greatest sense of achievement from walking around the holding with his family, knowing that he and Jacqueline have created something special for their children. After all, he says, 'We were inspired by Gandhi's words "Be the change you want to see in the world" and we do believe we have created something worth passing on to the kids. We believe that we must work as if we were farming for ever.'

Tinker's Bubble

Tinker's Bubble is a community smallholding set in 16 hectares (40 acres) of rural Somerset. It was established in 1994 by a group of people intent on living a low-impact lifestyle modelled, as member and land rights activist Simon Fairlie puts it, on a 'sustainable iron-age village'. Named after the spring that rises in the middle of the holding, Tinker's Bubble is an extraordinarily beautiful and diverse site, consisting of steep, dense woodland, sloping pasture and orchards. It took five years for the smallholding to get planning permission for twelve adults to live on the land they worked. Today, their operation provides subsistence and a low-cost, sustainable lifestyle for the inhabitants as well as commercial sales of vegetables and timber products.

Home and resources

The original dwellings at Tinker's Bubble were tents: now a small group of buildings, all made from local materials (mainly the Douglas Fir trees that dominate much of the woodland), are tucked away in the holding. A founding tenet of the Tinker's Bubble 'experiment' was that no fossil fuels should be used on the site, a constraint which has demanded low-technology solutions, particularly for the forestry operation. Trees are brought down by hand, then taken to the on-site sawmill by a Shire horse called Sam, who also works in the fields when needed (for example, at haymaking time). The logs are cut by a steam-powered saw, fuelled by waste wood taken from the site. Much of the agricultural work is done by human power, including the major task of cutting hay, which is done by hand with traditional scythes.

All heating is provided by wood; and cooking happens either on a wood stove in the communal roundhouse or outside on an open fire. The smallholding does use electricity, but only a fraction of what a single modern household would consume. There is no grid connection: the combination of a 750W wind turbine and 300W peak solar PV array, using batteries for storage, provides a supply of electricity through the year that is adequate for lighting, charging cordless tools and powering the odd laptop. There are no washing machines, televisions, dishwashers or other energy-guzzling paraphernalia of the modern world at Tinker's Bubble (although a battery-powered fridge gets occasional use in the hottest days of summer).

Tinker's Bubble is autonomous in water as well as energy. Although there is a mains connection, it isn't used: the spring provides all the holding's water needs, with a ram pump, powered by the spring's flow, taking water up to the main living area. Sewerage is dealt with locally by composting toilets and earth closets.

Economics

Most of the income at Tinker's Bubble currently comes from the sale of organic vegetables (at local markets) and timber products. There are also products from the substantial orchard: the apples themselves, then apple juice and cider. There are two Jersey cows, with calves, and a heifer: dairy products are also sold, but most of the dairy output is consumed on the holding. As much as possible, the livestock – the cows and their calves (who eventually go for beef) and the Shire horse – eat fodder produced on-site: fresh grass in the season and hay through the winter months. Organic lucerne is bought in to supplement the cows' feed.

Tinker's Bubble provides for all its members' basic needs for a cost per person of £23 per week. As Simon Fairlie points out: 'When people think about self-sufficiency, they tend to be thinking about growing your own vegetables. But that takes only a tiny fraction of someone's expenditure, maybe 1–2 per cent. Tinker's Bubble is self-sufficient in energy, water, housing, furniture, even entertainment: that's why it can cost relatively little for people to live like this.' Members still need to buy their own clothes, beer (although the holding is self-sufficient in cider!), private motor transport and luxuries, but the basics of life are catered for by the land.

This lifesyle comes at a price: the work is hard and physical, and the dynamics of community living don't suit everyone. But the rhythm of life at Tinker's Bubble – and the beautiful, biodiverse space it occupies – shows that genuinely sustainable rural development is not only possible, but attainable.

FURTHER READING

1 Growing your own food

Books

All About Compost, Pauline Pears, Search Press, 1999.

Grow Your Own Vegetables, Joy Larkcom, first published 1976 as Vegetables from Small Gardens, Frances Lincoln, 2002.

Encyclopaedia of Organic Gardening, Henry Doubleday Research Association, editor-in-chief Pauline Pears, Dorling Kindersley, 2001.

The River Cottage Cookbook, Hugh Fearnley-Whittingstall, HarperCollins, 2001.

Organic Gardening, Pauline Pears and Sue Stickland, Mitchell Beazley, 2000.

Soil, Charlie Ryrie, Gaia Books, 2001.

Pests, Charlie Ryrie, Gaia Books, 2001.

Compost, Charlie Ryrie, Gaia Books, 2001.

The Edible Container Garden, Michael Guerra, Gaia Books, 2005.

Internet publications and websites

Pesticides in your food, available from Pesticides Action Network, www.pan-uk.org

2 Raising your own food

Books

Guide to Bees and Honey, Ted Hooper, first published 1976, Marston House, 2001.

Bees at the Bottom of the Garden, Alan Campion, first published 1983, Alan Campion, 2001.

Keeping Traditional Pig Breeds: available from www.pigparadise.com

Starting with Chickens, Katie Thear, Broad Leys Publishing Ltd, 1999.

Internet publications and websites

British Beekeepers Association, www.bbka.org.uk – information and links to local beekeeping associations

Starting to keep domestic ducks, available from British Waterfowl Association, www.waterfowl.org.uk

Pigs: a guide for new keepers, Defra, available from www.defra.gov.uk

Keeping poultry, Low Impact Living Initiative, available from www.lowimpact.org

Too hard to swallow: the truth about drugs and poultry, Soil Association, available from www.soilassociation.org

3 Getting the most from your home harvest

Books
500 Recipes for Jams, Pickles, Chutneys, Marguerite Patten, Paul Hamlyn, 1963.

Internet publications and websites
Storage of organically produced crops, MAFF/HDRA, 1997, available from the
  Henry Doubleday Research Foundation at www.hdra.org.uk

4 Building biodiversity

Books
How to Make a Wildlife Garden, Chris Baines, Frances Lincoln, 2000.
Attracting Wildlife to Your Garden, Michael Chinery, Collins, 2004.

Internet publications and websites
Living Planet Report 2004, WWF, available from www.panda.org

6 Making your home more self-reliant

Books
The Whole House Book, Pat Borer and Cindy Harris, Centre for Alternative
  Technology Publications, 1998.
Lifting the Lid: an ecological approach to toilet systems, Peter Harper and
  Louise Halestrap, Centre for Alternative Technology Publications, 1999.

Internet publications and websites
Energy and Climate Change, Friends of the Earth, available from www.foe.org.uk
Small or atomic? Comparing the finances of nuclear and micro-generated energy,
  Green Alliance, available from www.green-alliance.org.uk
Eco-minimalism: getting the priorities right, Howard Liddell and Nick Grant,
  available from Elemental Solutions, www.elementalsolutions.co.uk
Eco-realism: an emerging paradigm?, Peter Harper, Centre for Alternative
  Technology, available from www.elementalsolutions.co.uk
The Nottingham Ecohome, www.msarch.co.uk/ecohome
Tree House, http://www.treehouseclapham.org.uk/
Micro-hydro power factsheet, Centre for Alternative Technology, can be
  purchased from www.cat.org.uk

Factsheets available from the Energy Saving Trust, at www.est.org.uk

Energy Efficient Refurbishment of Existing Housing
Advanced Insulation in Housing Refurbishment
Groundsource Heat Pumps
Biomass
Small Scale Wind Energy
Small Scale Hydroelectricity
Solar PV

Factsheets available from the Environment Agency, www.environment-agency.gov.uk

Conserving water in buildings
Harvesting rainwater for domestic use
Water efficient WCs and retrofits
Conserving water in buildings: domestic appliances
Conserving water in buildings: greywater
Conserving water in buildings: gardening

Micro-hydro power factsheet, CAT

7 Going all the way

Books
The Complete Book of Self-Sufficiency, John Seymour, first published 1975, Dorling Kindersley, 1996.
The Earth Care Manual, Patrick Whitefield, Permanent Publications, 2004.

Internet
Building your own energy efficient house, Energy Saving Trust, available from www.est.org.uk

Background reading: ecology, economics, food, politics

Gaia: a new look at life on Earth, first published 1979, James Lovelock, Oxford University Press, 2000.
Silent Spring, Rachel Carson, first published 1962, Penguin Classics, 2000.
Small is Beautiful, E. F. Schumacher, first published 1973, Vintage, 1993.
The One-Straw Revolution, Masanobu Fukuoka, first published 1978, Other India Press, 2004.
Permaculture One, Bill Mollison and David Holmgren, first published 1978, Tagari, 1990.
Not on the Label, Felicity Lawrence, Penguin, 2004.
Shopped, Joanna Blythman, Fourth Estate, 2004.
The Little Earth Book, James Bruges, Alastair Sawday Publishing, 2004.
Growth Fetish, Clive Hamilton, Pluto Press, 2003.